THE FIRST TIME HOME INVESTOR BOOK

Michael Wolf

LEADERS IN GLOBAL PUBLISHING

Published by Motivational Press, Inc.
7777 N Wickham Rd, # 12-247
Melbourne, FL 32940
www.MotivationalPress.com

Manufactured in the United States of America.

ISBN: 978-1-62865-094-5

Contents

FOREWORD

I KNOW OF NO SYSTEM OR PROGRAM THAT BY ITSELF CAN EDUCATE A REAL estate investor on how to become an overnight success, despite all the claims of, "get rich quick" investment programs and real estate coaching. Every single one of the successful real estate investors I know got that way through trial and error, plenty of error, and by surrounding themselves with the right people to guide them through the process, help them find deals, and structure them correctly. *The First Time Home Investor Book* introduces you to real estate investing and the benefits it can provide you with, but this is just the beginning. Mike Wolf doesn't introduce any new, revolutionary real estate tactic, he provides you with tried and tested investment strategies and principles that work, not just for him, but for the many repeat investor clients he works with on a consistent basis.

In his previous book, *The First Time Home Buyer Book*, Mike explains how to successfully navigate the real estate buying process for the first time. Now, Mike moves his readers from first time buyer to first time investor. The opportunity for real estate investors is better than ever, and this is the first book of its kind to literally walk you through, step-by-step, the process of becoming a successful investor with Mike by your side.

Real Estate education programs for first time investors have failed to build measurable success for 99% of potential investors, leaving most of them discouraged. As Mike points out, there are numerous types of investors, misconceptions first time investors have, and tax incentives investors need to be aware of. In short, a full awareness of the lessons, strategies, and tools Mike provides herein is the first step towards first time investor success.

Justin Sachs, Best Selling Author of *The Power of Persistence*
and *Ultimate Business Mastery*

PREFACE

"If you want to be independently rich and wealthy in real estate, I've found that you must work diligently at becoming a successful landlord of as many properties as possible."

– Michael Wolf

W HEN I WAS IN COLLEGE, MY BEST FRIEND AND I TEAMED UP WITH four other friends to rent a big house together. While rent was quite high where we went to college, teaming up allowed us to rent a nicer house at a reasonable cost for each of us. My best friend and I agreed to cut costs further by sharing a room and splitting the cost. That room was the garage—and oddly enough, we were not only totally OK with this setup, but thought it was the best thing ever! Both of us were paying $550 each. The garage was pulling in over $13,000 in rent each year for our landlord, not including the rent our other roommates were paying out each month. It was around this time I took note of what was going on around me involving real estate. I remember thinking that our landlord had a pretty sweet deal going on. He played in a Beatles cover band for weddings and Bar Mitzvahs, and the home we were renting was owned free and clear (there was no mortgage). Our rent for that house paid all of his bills and then some; the gigs he played for kicks on the weekend with his band brought in his "fun-money." I remember having an epiphany— and I cannot pinpoint the exact day due to my foggy recollection of the events that made up my college experience but it happened for sure. This changed the way I thought about real estate, wealth accumulation, cash flow, and most importantly, being able to live comfortably from the good decisions and investments made throughout life. From then on, I was focused on building wealth, and I knew this process would focus primarily on investment real estate.

Throughout history, if one group of society were considered generally more wealthy and successful in purely monetary terms, it would be landlords at the forefront of this list. Not all of the wealthiest people on the planet built their wealth primarily through real estate investment, but it is certain that nearly all of them utilize some form of investment real estate as a means to cultivate or protect their wealth as a cornerstone strategy for wealth management and preservation. It would seem that landlords in general are more likely to live a life of wealth and comfort throughout their lifetime. In fact, your average homeowner has thirty five times the net worth of the average renter[1]. There is an undeniable correlation between homeownership and wealth, and even more so, for those who are not just homeowners but landlords of investment property as well.

This book was written for the beginning real estate investor looking to become a landlord; someone who is ready to take the leap into becoming an owner of investment real estate. It's a roadmap to success with investment real estate, and it assumes that you already own your personal residence. If you don't already own your own home, consider learning from my other book, *The First Time Homebuyer Book*[2], to get you on the right path to wealth through homeownership before you skip straight to an investment property. Generally speaking, it's wise to have your personal home situation settled, owned, and in place before you consider owning investment property.

With that being said, one of the easiest ways for an average family or person to develop and grow a considerable net-worth has been through real estate ownership and investment property.

Investment real estate allows you to become the landlord instead of throwing your hard-earned money away by paying rent to cover a landlord's mortgage, and rather than putting all of your eggs in a structured financial investment basket of stocks and bonds. Renting to tenants will help you pay your own mortgage off, while the value of your real estate increases. It's a no-brainer.

---

[1]   http://goo.gl/v7F9ts; Shorewest Realtors – "Federal Reserve Study Reveals Homeowners Net Worth is over 30 Times Greater than Renters"

[2]   www.thefirsttimehomebuyerbook.com

It's a simple concept to comprehend, but it's not an easy process, and because of this, a vast majority of people fail or don't try to become an owner of real estate investment property. This book will help you get the knowledge and the confidence to take that next step into becoming a real estate investor. If you have the knowledge and the will power, you're very likely to succeed in your endeavors to becoming a landlord. And for that matter, you'll be part of the wealthiest segment of individuals throughout the globe. Experience rewards you within this process. The more you are involved and the more you invest, the wiser and wealthier you will become. Investing in yourself by purchasing and reading this book is the first step to becoming independently wealthy. It's my sincere goal to help you along this pathway to success that many should take, but few actually see all the way through.

I encourage you to delve into the content of the following pages. Highlight what connects with you and explore that in depth. Be courageous and know this text will be your general guide to purchasing investment real estate by learning through the stories and examples of clients we've already helped through the process. More than anything, you should know that there is no "one size fits all" process for real estate investors; everyone has different goals, dreams, means, and desires for their real estate aspirations. People have various budgets and many reasons behind their goals with investment property ownership. Nevertheless, allow this book to help find what resonates most for you in terms of the what, where, when, and why of real estate investing. Let it help you focus on what's most important for you and then go after it!

INTRODUCTION

"I'd Buy Up 'A Couple Hundred Thousand' Single Family Homes If I Could - I don't think we're remotely near a bubble now in terms of housing."[3]

–Warren Buffett

Our housing market is in the rebound stage and we are appreciating throughout the United States.. We're currently in a positive appreciation cycle in the real estate market with opportunities for everyone who can seize the potential at hand. There have been, and will continue to be, several real estate booms and busts throughout history: natural ebbs and flows to the market and seasons of change. In terms of where we stand today, after so many consecutive years of negativity in values, as well as the general outlook of the housing market, real estate in the United States is on sale and poised to become one of, if not the best market segments to invest your time and money for the foreseeable future. The stock market is, and can be great, but it may not be the Holy Grail to your wealth and retirement. Financial advisors are always quick to tell you to invest in the financial markets and will hardly ever broach the topic of investment real estate. I would tell you to make the most out of both your real estate holdings and other financial investments, but do so in accordance with your risk profile and overall life goals. Investment property can offer so much more than your typical financial market investments (stocks, bonds, and mutual funds). You cannot live inside your stock that you purchase or own. You cannot build "sweat-equity" in it over and above what you paid for the stock. You cannot create the tax shelters within a stock investment that a real estate investment has the ability to offer. After reading this book, you should be in a position to

3   http://www.dailyfinance.com/2013/05/12/63-brand-new-quotes-from-warren-buffett/ and http://www.cnbc.com/id/46538421

take advantage of the current market trends. You will have been educated with the knowledge of who, what, why, when, where, and how, in terms of your first real estate investment. In conjunction with my first book, *The First Time Homebuyer Book*, you will gain expanded knowledge from a professional that has assisted hundreds of clients, rather than blazing your own trail and learning through your own potentially costly and timely mistakes. In regards to real estate investments, you will learn from experiences in this book, what to do, what not to do, and everything in between.

With the housing market in a recovery stage, many people have begun to think of how they can take advantage of opportunities in the current market. Many of these people already own their own residence, so the focus is being placed squarely on investment property as a real estate goal for the foreseeable future. Real estate, as an investment, presents several great opportunities with relatively limited risk. If you buy with the best practices and investing principals presented in this book, you will be able to take advantage and cash in on the best opportunities that exist in the advantageously positioned current market cycle of real estate. Good things are truly in store for our future.

The majority of people out there would love to consider investing in real estate but don't know where to start. This book was written to give you a great foundation of knowledge on how to correctly plan, search, analyze, and purchase your first real estate investment. Hopefully, it's the first of many, and the beginning of your real estate empire in its own right.

Economic success is squarely in your own hands. The end result is based on the summation of the effort that you put in along the way. This is especially true for real estate investing, as with any other form of investment. All else being equal, the more time and effort you put in, the better the result in the end. Of course, you should try to get the best people to help you along the way like a great real estate agent and a lending professional, but you cannot rely on these people to do all the work. Most people reading this book will have a retirement fund or plan of some sort. I am willing to bet, the return on the retirement portfolio correlates with the specific amount of time that you personally put into it. Like most people, not a lot of time is put into their actual retirement investments, when it comes to analyzing and overseeing what you are investing (or invested) in. Therefore, the returns you are realizing are probably average. Through this process of investing in real estate, you will definitely want to lean on your professional advisors and real estate professionals for guidance and assistance. However, you'll also want to be as involved as possible, so you can make the important decisions with confidence by utilizing the tools and concepts you've learned in this book. We will help expand your knowledge of the right things to look for, the best questions to ask, potential issues, and pitfalls to be aware of throughout the process of finding the right real estate investment for you. You can have the best team and resources at your disposal, but without your effort and oversight with your goals in mind, the possibility for a mistake or poor judgment will increase, potentially leading you away from your goal.

Don't be afraid to get immersed in the process. The more questions you ask and the more involved you are, the better the result, and the better prepared you will be for the next property. This should be a fun and exciting process. With the right mindset, you should be prepared to address any hurdle or pitfall that may arise, making sure to stay cool, calm, and collected all the way to the close of escrow of your first investment property.

Throughout the course of this book, I will introduce you to several time-tested concepts and provide a variety of tips and strategies to assist you in this first time real estate investment purchase. Everything presented has been field tested, implemented, and refined in the trenches of the day-to-day dealings for our business and our clients. Some of these tips and strategies will involve tax and/or legal (ownership) implications. Furthermore, we operate out of Southern California, and although the main concepts of the book can be applied globally, all real estate is indeed local and indicative of the local trends and acceptable practices. Therefore, what is or may be common for the areas I operate from, may not be exactly the same for you. However, for the integrity of this book, I've done my best to offer the fundamentals that can provide a solid base of understanding, so you can apply the best strategies and tactics whether you are in California, Florida, or anywhere in between. As always, you should consult your tax or legal professional when it comes to issues of tax or manner of holding title, and I promise to keep the legal disclaimers to a minimum.

Mastery of a subject always begins somewhere. "A journey of a thousand miles must begin with a single step." Every professional started as a rookie, where they knew little to nothing about the subject at hand. The difference between greatness and everyone else is that the people who become great go after their goal(s) with a burning desire for success; they do so by out-caring and out-working the competition, and executing plans with sincerity and integrity. If your goal is to own your first or many real estate investments, I commend you for giving yourself a great launching pad by reading this book. Devour the pages—they are the basics and fundamentals set forth in an easy to understand manner so that you can apply them towards your first investment purchase. Refine these skills as you go through the purchase and subsequent purchases thereafter.

When given the opportunity to display their knowledge of the process at hand, many of our clients witness first-hand how much better their transaction is. There's a high level of overall comprehension, which makes communication and satisfaction of the end result much more likely. Not only will you be better understood by everyone involved in your purchase, you will also have a better understanding to know what is really happening (reading between the lines), acknowledging and noticing a potential issue or problem before it gets out of control (awareness), and knowing the right questions to ask throughout the process (competence and knowledge). By reading this book, you're arming yourself with a solid understanding of the main tenants of what makes for a decent investment, and a great overview of the methods of which to attain an excellent real estate investment property; the sky's the limit after that. If a journey of a thousand miles begins with a single step, it is my wish that you take the first step in confidence with this book in hand. Here's to you, and to the best of luck with your future real estate investments and overall success.

"Every dollar spent today, is a dollar that cannot be invested for the future. Every dollar invested today, is a dollar that cannot be spent on instant gratification. The world is full of people who may talk the talk, but when it gets right down to the decision, they will not invest. They simply do not have the discipline to restrict some of their current spending in order to invest, or they simply are not risk takers."

-Dennis Mackenzie

Part I

The Theory of Real Estate Investment

How Investment Real Estate is Part of a
Healthy Equation for Wealth

CHAPTER 1

Why Should You have Investment Real Estate in the First Place?

ECAUSE IT'S THE *IDEAL* INVESTMENT! INVESTMENT REAL ESTATE isn't for everyone, and we will cover that in the next chapter. But let's take a moment to address the reasons why people should have investment real estate in the first place. The easiest answer is a well-known acronym that addresses the key benefits for all investment real estate. Put simply, Investment Real Estate is an IDEAL investment.[4] The IDEAL stands for:

- I – Income

- D – Depreciation

- E – Expenses

- A – Appreciation

- L – Leverage

Real estate is the IDEAL investment compared to all others. I'll explain each benefit in depth.

"I" stands for **Income** (a.k.a. positive cash flow): Your investment property should be generating income from rent received each month. Of course, there will be months where you may experience a vacancy, but for the most part your investments will be producing an income. Be careful because many times beginning investors exaggerate their assumptions and don't take into account all potential costs. The investor should know going into the purchase that the property will COST money each month

---

[4] Author's Note: The IDEAL acronym is commonly known and taught and cannot be properly credited by one source or entity.

(known as negative cash flow). This scenario, although not ideal, may be OK, only in specific instances that we will discuss later. It boils down to risk tolerance and the ability of the owner to fund and pay for a negative producing asset. In the boom years of real estate, prices were sky high and the rents didn't increase proportionately with many residential real estate investment properties. Many naïve investors purchased properties with the assumption that the appreciation in prices would more than compensate for the fact that the high balance mortgage would be a significant negative impact on the funds each month. Be aware of this and do your best to forecast a positive cash flow scenario, so that you can actually realize the INCOME part of the IDEAL equation. We will discuss forecasting and how to do so later on in the book. Often times, it may require a higher down payment (therefore lesser amount being mortgaged) so that your cash flow is acceptable each month. Ideally, you eventually pay off the mortgage so there is no question that cash flow will be coming in each month, and substantially so. This ought to be a vital component to one's retirement plan. Do this a few times and you won't have to worry about money later on down the road, which is the main goal of this book as well as the reward for taking the risk in purchasing investment property in the first place.

"D" stands for **Depreciation**: With investment real estate, you are able to utilize its depreciation for your own tax benefit. What is depreciation anyway? It's a non-cost accounting method to take into account the overall financial burden incurred through real estate investment. Look at this another way, when you buy a brand new car, the minute you drive off the lot, that car has depreciated in value. When it comes to your investment real estate property, the IRS allows you to deduct this amount yearly against your taxes.[5]

I am not a tax professional, so this is not meant to be a lesson in taxation policy or to be construed as tax advice. With that said, the depreciation of a real estate investment property is determined by the overall value of the structure, of the property, and the length of time (recovery period based on the property type—either residential or commercial). If you have ever

---

[5] http://goo.gl/8hRwns 2012 Publication 946 - Internal Revenue Service

gotten a property tax bill, they usually break your property's assessed value into two categories: one for the value of the land, and the other for the value of the structure. Both of these values added up equals your total "basis" for property taxation. When it comes to depreciation, you can deduct against your taxes on the original base value of the structure only; the IRS doesn't allow you to depreciate land value (because land is typically only appreciating). Just like your new car driving off the lot, it's the structure on the property that is getting less and less valuable every year as its effective age gets older and older. And you can use this to your tax advantage.

The best example of the benefit regarding this concept is through depreciation, you can actually turn a property that creates a positive cash flow into one that shows a loss (on paper) when dealing with taxes and the IRS. By doing so, that (paper) loss is deductible against your income for tax purposes. Therefore, it's a great benefit for people that are specifically looking for a "tax-shelter" of sorts for their real estate investments.

For example, and without getting too technical, assume that you are able to depreciate $15,000 a year from a $500,000 residential investment property that you own. Let's say that you are cash-flowing $1,000 a month (meaning that after all expenses, you are net-positive $1,000 each month), so you have $12,000 total annual income for the year from this property's rental income. Although you took in $12,000, you can show through your accountancy with the depreciation of the investment real estate that you actually lost $3,000 on paper, which is used against any income taxes that you may owe. From the standpoint of the IRS, this property realized a loss of $3,000 after the "expense" of the $15,000 depreciation amount was taken into account. Not only are there no taxes due on that rental income, you can utilize the paper loss of $3,000 against your other regular taxable income from your day-job. Investment property at higher price points will have proportionally higher tax-shelter qualities. Investors use this to their benefit in being able to deduct as much against their taxable amount owed each year through the benefit of depreciation with their underlying real estate investment.

Although this is a vastly important benefit to owning investment real estate, the subject is not well understood. Because depreciation is a somewhat complicated tax subject, the above explanation was meant to be cursory in nature. When it comes to issues involving taxes and depreciation, make sure you have a tax professional that can advise you appropriately so you know where you stand.

"E" stands for **Expenses**: Generally, all expenses incurred relating to the property are deductible when it comes to your investment property. The cost for utilities, the cost for insurance, the mortgage, and the interest and property taxes you pay. If you use a property manager or if you're repairing or improving the property itself, all of this is deductible. Real estate investment comes with a lot of expenses, duties, and responsibilities to ensure the investment property itself performs to its highest capability. Because of this, contemporary tax law generally allows that all of these related expenses are deductible to the benefit of the investment real estate landowner. If you were to take a loss, or purposefully took a loss on a business investment or investment property, that loss (or expense) can carry over for multiple years against your income taxes. For some people, this is an aggressive and technical strategy. Yet, it's another potential benefit of investment real estate.

	Homeowner	Investor
Deductions During Ownership	• loan interest; • property taxes.	• All operating expenses • Depreciation
Exemptions Upon Sale	Special exemption from capital gain taxation up to designated a mounts.	Must pay taxes on capital gains unless the transaction is set up as a tax deferred 1031 exchange

Quick Comparison: Deductions & Exemptions between an owner-occupied vs. investment property:

"**A**" stands for **Appreciation**: Appreciation means, the growth of value of the underlying investment. It's one of the main reasons that we invest in the first place, and it's a powerful way to grow your net worth. Many homes in the city of San Francisco are several million dollars in today's market, but back in the 1960s, the same property was worth about the cost of the car you are currently driving (probably even less!). Throughout the years, the area became more popular and the demand that ensued caused the real estate prices in the city to grow exponentially compared to where they were a few decades ago. People who were lucky enough to recognize this, or were just in the right place at the right time and continued to live in their home, have realized an investment return in the 1000's of percent. Now that's what appreciation is all about. What other investment can make you this kind of return without drastically increased risk? The best part about investment real estate is that someone is paying you to live in your property, paying off your mortgage, and creating an income (positive cash flow) for you each month along the way throughout your course of ownership.

"**L**" stands for **Leverage**: Many people refer to this as "OPM" (other people's money). This is when you are using a small amount of your money to control a much more expensive asset. You are essentially leveraging your down payment and gaining control of an asset that you would normally not be able to purchase without the loan itself. Leverage is much more acceptable in the real estate world and inherently less risky than leverage in the stock world (where this is done through means of options or buying "on Margin"). Leverage is common in real estate. Otherwise, people would only buy property when they had 100% of the cash to do so. Over a third of all purchases are all-cash transactions as our recovery continues.[6] Still, about 2/3 of all purchases are done with some level of financing, so the majority of buyers in the market enjoy the power that leverage can offer when it comes to investment real estate.

For example, if a real estate investor was to buy a house that costs $100,000 with 10% down payment, they are leveraging the remaining

---

[6] http://www.marketwatch.com/story/nearly-half-of-all-homes-are-purchased-in-cash-2013-08-29

90% through the use of the associated mortgage. Let's say the local market improves by 20% over the next year, and therefore the actual property is now worth $120,000. When it comes to leverage, from the standpoint of this property, its value increased by 20%. But compared to the investor's actual down payment (the "skin in the game") of $10,000— this increase in property value of 20% really means the investor doubled their return on the investment actually made—also known as the "cash-on-cash" return. In this case, that is 200%—because the $10,000 is now responsible and entitled to a $20,000 increase in overall value and the overall potential profit.

Quick Definition - Cash-on-Cash Return:

A calculation that determines the cash income on the cash invested. Cash-on-cash return would measure the annual return you made on the property in relation to the down payment.[7]

Although leverage is considered a benefit, like everything else, there can always be too much of a good thing. In 2007, when the real estate market took a turn for the worst, many investors were over-leveraged and fared the worst. They could not weather the storm of a correcting economy. As we will discuss further within the book, exercising caution with every investment made will help to ensure that you can purchase, retain, pay-off debt, and grow your wealth from the investment decisions made, as opposed to being at the mercy and whim of the overall market fluctuations. Surely, as the past would dictate, there will be future booms and busts as we continue to move forward. The more planning and preparing done while building net worth will help prevent us from being bruised and battered by the side effects of whatever market we find ourselves in.

Many people think that investment real estate is only about cash flow and appreciation, but it's so much more than that. As mentioned above, you can realize several benefits through each real estate investment property you purchase. The challenge is to maximize the benefits through every investment.

---

[7] http://www.investopedia.com/terms/c/cashoncashreturn.asp

Furthermore, the **IDEAL** acronym is not just a reminder of the benefits of investment real estate; it's also here to serve as a guide for every investment property you will consider purchasing in the future. Any property you purchase should conform to all of the letters that represent the IDEAL acronym. The underlying property should have a good reason for not fitting all the guidelines. In almost every case, if there is an investment you are considering that doesn't hit all the guidelines, by most accounts you should probably PASS on it!

Take for example a story of my own, regarding a property that I purchased early on in my real estate career. To this day, it's the biggest investment mistake that I've made, and it's precisely because I didn't follow the IDEAL guidelines that you are reading and learning about now. I was naïve and my experience was not yet fully developed. The property I purchased was a vacant lot in a gated community development. The property already had an HOA (a monthly maintenance fee) because of the nice amenity facilities that were built for it and in anticipation of would-be-built homes. There were high expectations for the future appreciation potential—but then, the market turned for the worse as we headed into the great recession that lasted from 2007-2012. Can you see what parts of the IDEAL guidelines I missed on completely? Let's start with "I". The vacant lot made no income! Sometimes this can be acceptable, if the deal is something that cannot be missed, but for the most part this deal was nothing special. In all honesty, I considered selling the trees that are currently on the vacant lot to the local wood mill for some actual income, or putting up a camping spot ad on the local Craigslist; but unfortunately, the lumber isn't worth enough and there are better spots to camp! My expectations and desire for price appreciation blocked the rational and logical questions that needed to be asked. So, when it came to the income aspect of the IDEAL guidelines for a real estate investment, I paid no attention to it. And I paid the price for my hubris. Furthermore, this investment failed to realize the benefit of depreciation as you cannot depreciate land! Therefore, we are zero for two so far with the IDEAL guideline to real estate investing. All I can do is hope the land appreciates to a point where it can be sold one day. Let's call it an expensive learning lesson. You too will have these "learning lessons"; just try to have as few of them as possible and you will be better off. Take from my experiences and the others that will be shared throughout this book to help you save time, money, hassle, and heartache. When it comes to making the most of your real estate investments, ALWAYS keep the IDEAL guideline in mind to make certain you are making a good decision and a solid investment.

CHAPTER 2

Fantastically important concepts for beginning investors:

"Invest in yourself. Your career is the engine of your wealth."

- Paul Clitheroe

AS YOU CONTINUE READING THROUGH THE FOLLOWING CHAPTERS, we will be breaking things down to types of investors, specific property types that we invest in, as well as the potential hurdles to avoid throughout your investment purchase adventure. With that in mind, there are a few key points—cornerstone foundational concepts— that every real estate investor should keep in mind. The investor often learns these concepts after making a mistake, or several mistakes. Hopefully, by reading these concepts you can apply them in real time and keep them in the back of your mind as you move through each stage of your investment process.

Investor Concept #1: When investing, keep the IDEAL investment concepts in mind. Although I already explained this in depth, it's important nonetheless to keep the IDEAL acronym guideline handy as it has saved me, and countless others, from making poor investment decisions. Using the IDEAL concept as a checklist of sorts, you can determine the strengths, weaknesses, opportunities, and threats that can make a potential investment attractive or unattractive. Use it with every opportunity and potential purchase that comes your way or that you are considering.

Investor Concept #2: Whenever looking for and considering an investment, keep in mind that *cash flow will not make you rich.* In other words, it would not be wise to depend solely on cash flow to create considerable wealth. There is no doubt the cash flow a property generates is a benefit of an investment—it's essentially an incentive, or benefit to the investor; it's the "glue" that will keep a deal together. If there was no cash flow, investors would have a hard time dealing with no return on the investment, and relying solely on the appreciation of the underlying property to perform and make the investment a good one. For example, if you are renting out an investment property for $2,000 a month, and your expenses are $1,800, then you are looking at a $200 per month cash flow. This is great, but sometimes it may take you a month or two to find a new tenant after one moves out, or, the roof begins to leak and you need to put a new roof on the house. There are countless other examples of what could happen. If anything like this happens throughout your ownership (and it certainly will), it could mean that all the cash flow you have been taking in throughout the year becomes spent on unexpected or non-normal expenses. In this example, just one month of vacancy means the equivalent of nine months' worth of cash flow , just to cover the monthly expenses and mortgage (expenses at $1,800 with a $200 per month cash flow). For this reason, you need to purchase with appreciation in mind and never buy an investment solely for the cash flow. I'll cover this in the next chapter. Even still, some investors will buy and hold in anticipation of future appreciation and never rely on cash flow (or income) coming in. This is especially true for a second home purchase or even a land purchase, where it would be unlikely for the owner to realize income from renting the place out.

Just because a property is cheap, doesn't mean it's a good investment. In California, a home can cost $500,000, when you can get a newer and bigger home in Texas for $120,000. Although you may be able to find cheaper investment properties elsewhere throughout the country, and even get a good cash flow, you must ask yourself what is the ceiling for appreciation? How high can it go? How high should it go relative to your other opportunities? Why invest in a home that can only appreciate so much, when you may have the opportunity to buy another more expensive home with the potential of doubling in value in the near future?

Investor Concept #3: Don't fall in love with a house until you have the keys in hand. A wise real estate investor once said that we (humans) "buy emotionally and later justify logically," when it comes to buying real estate. At the core of any purchase is some element of an emotional push to say "yes." Even the staunchest and most emotionless of investors can get caught up with the sentimental or emotional tug-o-war that occurs when they find a property they love. Whenever you fall in love with a place, emotions may take over and cause you to effectively lose any leverage you may have at the negotiation table. Once it's clear that you love the place, the other agent or seller will know that you will do what it takes to make this place yours. They will use it against you through the inspection period, if there are items that you request a credit for or to be repaired. When it comes to the negotiation of the purchase and throughout the process of the transaction, never fall in love until it's yours. It's a good rule of thumb to be able to walk away from the transaction, no matter how hard it may seem. In fact, the walk away may very well be your best leverage and negotiation tactic as a buyer. You can use the "walk away" in negotiation, and the fear of losing you as the potential buyer may motivate the seller to act, in your favor.

Investor Concept #4: Don't focus just on the curb appeal, focus on the FINANCIAL$—Put a good deal of weight with your decision after reviewing and verifying the numbers. Sometimes I see many first-time investors being caught up with the curb appeal of the investment property that they are thinking of buying. To some extent, this is important, but I always tend to remind these investor buyers that *they are not going to be living in this home and what you are buying is a cash machine—it doesn't necessarily need to be a pretty one.* The curb appeal isn't as important as you may think, as long as the income the property generates makes up for whatever inadequacies there are in the curb appeal. So what if the place looks less than optimal? If it's generating a return that is equal to or greater than other properties that are nearby but at a lesser price point, then it's a great deal and investment. Not only are you able to get this place for a good value, you may be able to increase rents by investing separately into the property after the sale by giving the curb appeal a "face lift" through cosmetic improvements. On the other hand, curb appeal to some extent is important to consider, if it would make a difference by turning off a potential tenant from even wanting to see the inside of the property. For the most part, however, being caught up with a property's curb appeal is a beginner investor's mistake, because you are failing to focus and take into account the investment return of the actual property itself. One strategy is to look for the ugly duckling that is making a solid rent. Use its "ugliness" to your advantage in negotiating with the seller. Then, invest into the property and increase rents and overall cash flow, while holding long enough for substantial appreciation—that's a winning way to go about your first investment property.

Investor Concept #5: Lean on your professionals. It is difficult to go it alone. Why would you? You want to lean on all of your professionals throughout this adventure to help you get to where you want to be, in a more efficient manner. Success is easier when you have a team of professionals on your side. This would certainly include your real estate professional as well as your loan professional. If you become more and more involved with the investment process, you will be able to assemble a greater network of individuals to assist you with every transaction—your Power team, but first things first. In order to become great, you need to get good. Start small, with finding or effectively utilizing your real estate and loan professional to the most extent possible. If you have good professionals, they should have their own power team of sorts. These would include inspectors, contractors, appraisers, financial experts, plumbers, electricians, roofers, etc. Lean on these professionals so that you don't have to go and reinvent the wheel with your team. This is how you should operate until you are successful enough that you are doing several investment deals a year. Then, you'll be able to assemble your own power team. Furthermore, it's important to know that your agent won't be doing all the work for you—you cannot expect that—the concept here is to *lean* on your professionals and not rely on them completely. By this, I mean that you need to be ready and prepared to do the legwork on the property by reviewing and studying the paperwork surrounding the transaction (which includes contracts, disclosures, finances, and other reports). Ultimately, it's your investment property. Therefore, the responsibility lies on you to make sure that after your research and number crunching, the investment will work for you, your budget, your family, and your overall investment goals. Once you've purchased the property, what's done is done; you've baked the cake and you can't return the flour. The professionals you have working for you will and should be doing a great job. However, once the place is sold and you are the new investor owner, they won't be around for the day-to-day nitty gritty details of investment-homeownership. You will be the CEO of this investment, so, you should make sure that you do absolutely everything possible to ensure you feel good about the investment; that it makes sense numbers-wise and fits within your budget.

Investor Concept #6: Novice investors serially underestimate everything. It happens with anything that you are not used to. It's easy to underestimate the time it takes to do a task you've never done before, or look up at a large hill and think you can get to the top in a couple of minutes. Remain cautious and conservative when it comes to all of the aspects of the investment process. You will soon find that a lot of the upfront work requires a good deal of assumptions and estimations. When you make these assumptions, be conservative. WARNING: Don't read this and think you need to go overboard with the conservatism. Too much of it is not a good thing, and you will find that you may exhibit the signs of what I call, "analysis paralysis." With that being said, many investors tend to underestimate the overall expenses for an investment property. They tend to underestimate the total cost of repairs that need to be made, or expect the investment property to be rented (not-vacant) 100% of the time.

Maintenance items can be a big unexpected cost, which is why it's important to be as prepared as possible. Do the research into the process and overall costs of any improvements a property will need. You will no doubt experience costs for this constant upkeep as the investor-owner, and it's important to properly budget in expectation and anticipation of maintenance expenses. Once you have an accepted offer and a property in escrow, your property inspector can help highlight the most pressing items, which usually come up during the inspection for the property, and from there, your agent can help you get in touch with specific professionals to find out the total cost of the repairs that will be needed, if any. The more prepared you are, the better you will be at managing your investment and preparing for unexpected costs. They will occur, so it's best to be ready for them. Otherwise, they will serve to destroy your financial predictions of the overall investment. Don't be discouraged because nearly every property has deferred maintenance. Sometimes the sellers know about it and they choose not to do anything, and sometimes the issues you find during an inspection are unknown.

You can do your best to negotiate repairs or credits for the issues that come about during your purchase transaction, but there's no guarantee the sellers will agree to your request. You'll also want to research how much it costs to operate a given investment property by comparing it to others, when you review enough of them (or at least the ones that list their expenses upfront), you will begin to see patterns of expenses. Sometimes the agent or seller doesn't list them. If it's a single family home, try calling the utility company to get the average use charges for a given-sized home, or for the exact one you are considering—if they'll give you that information. Through research and comparison, you can see that for a four-unit building, the cost for utilities, maintenance, pest control, or trash is a given number. From that number, you can estimate the cost for a two-unit property by dividing it in half. Making these calculated estimated assumptions upfront will help identify the best property on the market for you to write an offer on. From there, you will want to verify all the numbers while in escrow, as the seller will be obligated to provide the financials. Then you can ensure they fit within the guidelines of what you were expecting when you made the offer.

CHAPTER 3

Who should buy investment property?

The "Who": The types of investors that exist in the market and determining if real estate investing is a good fit for you.

> "Despite abundant advertisements claiming that real estate investing is an easy way to wealth, it is in fact a challenging business requiring expertise, planning, and focus." [8]

Jean Folger

Perhaps I should have started the book with this chapter—Is real estate investing right for you in the first place? Buying investment property is not a simple walk in the park. Do you remember the spectrum of emotions that you experienced when you purchased your first house? More often than not beginner, and sometimes even professionalreal estate investors get lost in the emotions of the purchase. After all, every purchase we make is an emotional decision that is later justified logically. This chapter will address the type of person that's compatible with investment real estate and who it won't work for as well. It will also address the different "flavors" of investors out there. If you are going to be a real estate investor, you will no doubt want to specialize in a certain niche or gain experience and eventually master being an investor of a specific type. My suggestion is to isolate the type you feel you relate with the most and really delve in and go for it. The more time and effort you put into your goal, the better the outcome. That's for sure.

---

[8]   http://www.forbes.com/2010/09/21/real-estate-investor-personal-finance-effective-habits.html

When it comes to investing in real estate, who wouldn't this work for? Well, if you are risk averse, then investing in real estate may not jive with you. Many risks, liabilities, and decisions need to be made and assumed. Nothing is ever 100% known or guaranteed; sometimes this element of the unknown is too much for some people to handle. Perhaps you are better off safeguarding your dollars by investing your money in a bond, a CD, or in gold. Essentially, there are certain people that just can't take the pressure, the expectations of a buyer, or the liability and responsibility of being a landlord. They cannot imagine making the decisions that need to be made, not just though the purchase process, but also throughout the course of ownership as well. The risk averse, the "worry-warts," and the "nervous-nellies" of the world just may not be able to handle the process of a real estate investment transaction without much stress and potential aggravation, especially on those assisting or along for the ride. Aside from not having the energy and wherewithal to withstand the deal, here are some of the most common negative factors that must be taken into account when it comes to investment real estate:

- **Liability**: It goes without saying that if you own property and you're renting it out, you are going to be taking on added liability. If something goes wrong, if someone gets hurt, you can be held responsible for it as the landlord and owner. Cash flow is fun until someone gets hurt, right? Conversely, for example, if you are investing in a bond there is a firmly knowable and concrete downside (the loss of all your money). Albeit unlikely, this is viewed as finite risk and no liability.

There are ways to protect yourself legally, especially if you are a high-wealth individual. These strategies should be part of a conversation that you have with your asset-protection attorney, but we will address some of the very basics in the book. What I've seen and what works in dealing with our high net worth investors is that they own their investment real estate in an LLC, or several LLC's. If something was to happen where there was a resulting lawsuit on a property and you were the owner, then your liability is contained within the contents of the assets in the LLC itself. In other words, if you get sued by a renter on your investment property that's owned in a specific LLC and they win the lawsuit, then they can only access what is owned in that specific LLC. And if the rental property is the only thing that's owned in the LLC, then you contain your losses (all generally speaking), while maintaining your other personal assets intact. If you become wealthy enough, or if you build a portfolio of several real estate properties, as mentioned before, you may want to own different investment property in several LLC's. I am getting ahead of myself, but know that there are specific options and a winning playbook for investment property ownership.

- **Being a Landlord** – Being a landlord entails responsibility, time, and energy towards the suitable management of your investment property. You can even have a property manager on hand, but you still need to allocate some time to insure that your property is performing as intended. If you aren't willing to take the time and make the commitment for the responsibility entailed in being a landlord, then this gig may not be for you.

- **Guarantee? There is none.** Real estate investment has inherent risks, but we know that there is less and less earth available as the population continues to expand. It's my personal opinion through my research that although landlords have gotten a lot of flak throughout history, it's because the landlords of the world have been realizing the greatest amount of wealth for generations. Sometimes accidents happen, markets detract, and properties stay vacant. These things can happen and you need to weigh the costs vs. the benefits before you decide to make the determination that investment property ownership is for you. Please make this determination before looking at property.

- **Difficulty to qualify for other home investments** – Although this may not play much of a factor, having investment property (or properties) can affect your ability to qualify for other investment property or other homes that you may wish to get financing for in order to buy. Plan accordingly and prepare as soon as possible—perhaps your first call should be to your loan officer to ensure there are no issues or areas of concern with financing and your future plans.

If you have made it this far, then you are probably shrugging off the above risks and barriers to becoming an investment property owner as no big deal. If it is a big deal, figure out whatever is concerning you now before moving forward. If the risks don't line up and you don't feel you would be comfortable with being a real estate investment owner, please pass this book along to someone you think it would benefit so we can help them too.

Types of Investors - specialty and mastery of your chosen investment niche:

When it comes to the different kinds of investors out there, you will find that there are several to choose from. Your end goal within the investment itself will determine the type of niche you find yourself operating in. The best advice would be to pick the niche that most resonates with you and become a master at it. Surely, this will all but solidify your path to success.

So what are the most common investor niches?

Buy and Hold – This is an investment where you are buying now to hold for a specific period of time. You can either rent your place out (buy and rent—I'll discuss this further below), or if you have the monetary funds or means to do so, which many second home or vacation home investors do, they purchase and hold without really meaning or needing to rent the place. This niche puts its emphasis solely on the appreciation of the investment over time. Location and value play an important role in this niche, and this purchase is really like buying another home where the rental potential and return on investment (in terms of monthly cash flow) are not as important as the likability and feeling (and of course the appreciation expectation) of the overall home itself. Beach property is a prime example of this kind of investment property. Coastal or beach property is an ideal location for an investor's second home or vacation home, and because this kind of property tends to hold its value and appreciate more than other locations. It's the quintessential kind of property to buy and hold. Generally, investors purchasing beach property have the wealth to hold the property and own it without the need to rent it out—many times, they don't want to rent it out because doing so will bring on more "wear and tear" on the property. For cash flow reasons, most investors don't find this property niche realistic, but it's sure nice to imagine as a possible end goal that you may want to work towards in your path to overall investment success.

Buy and Rent – This is the most common form of investment property. This is like buy and hold except that there is a specific intent to rent the property out. Whether it's a vacation/seasonal rental or a residential rental property, the rent-ability aspect of the property is of primary importance. The investor is hoping the property appreciates over time. In the meantime, the property should be cash flowing monthly to address any expenses or fix up costs that may be required to manage the property throughout the course of ownership. In this equation, you're the landlord, so you should be prepared to handle all the tasks and expectations that come with it.

BONUS: Later in the book, we'll discuss specific strategies and tactics that you can implement as a landlord. And how small, inexpensive, and unexpected extras can work to enhance the type of tenant you rent out to. This will have a positive effect on your investment property. Always remember: *Happy tenants, happy property—and vice versa.*

If you manage your property well, and it's a nice place to live, you can expect to get the highest rents that your property can command. If the place you are considering is a few shades away from "slumlord" status, then you can expect to rent out to less than stellar tenants at less than stellar rents. Good advice: treat the tenants as you would want to be treated and your property will be the benefactor from this symbiotic relationship.

When it comes to buy and rent, the numbers are very important. How much does the unit(s) rent out for? Is there room for improvement (compared to what other similar units are renting for in the area)? How much deferred maintenance is there? What fix-up costs must be done now and which can be held off over time? What are the drawbacks to renting this place out, if any?

For any property you are looking to invest in, both subjective and objective analysis should be taken into consideration. Subjectively, you want to consider resale potential and ability—is there anything that could prevent an easy resale? You'll want to consider the neighborhood and the property's location—is it on a busy street? Is it convenient for public transport access? Is the area considered a "walkable" neighborhood, in your opinion? Is it near an area that will be developed or re-developed to the benefit (or detriment) to your property at hand? You should be asking yourself these questions. Be curious and think long-term. Objectively, you will want to analyze the financials—the income versus the expenses.

BONUS: In the resource section at the end of this book, we'll provide information that will help you analyze investment property, project cash flows, and project rents, all to help you to make the best most logical decision for your investment at hand.

The majority of investors out there are investing in property with the intention of buying and then renting the property out. This process is fairly easy to manage and maintain. The risk and downside is limited and the process is simple. The hardest part is getting (purchasing) the property in the first place.

A word about getting started, before you begin looking at property: get preapproved.

Before you even go looking at or inside a property, you should talk to a loan professional for financing options. Ideally, your loan professional will consistently work with investors or specialize in working with investors, like yourself. If you don't have a great loan officer professional, you may want to consult your realtor professional to see if they have a referral for you. If you don't have a Realtor professional that you can consult, consider asking a friend or family member that recently had a great experience with their Realtor. Alternatively, as a bonus of purchasing this book, you can consult the resource section at the end of the book; we can source for you a great professional lender or Realtor through our nationwide network of professionals. It's so important to work with a professional Realtor, and we certainly have you covered in this perspective. We can get you hooked up with a great professional Realtor that can help you get to the finish line faster, with as little hassle and heartache as possible. When it comes to something as important as what your Realtor professional does, there is no time for a second chance. It's better to work with a professional with a great track record and experience as opposed to a family member who has their real estate license.

BONUS: There is no need to pick someone randomly from the internet. If you don't already have one, we can help you get linked up with someone. This is an important decision in your investment process, so you need to be confident in the professional assisting you.

Unless you are all cash, meaning you don't need a loan or financing for your purchase, you must focus on your qualification ability as well. You need to find out what you can qualify for in terms of your investment property for the following two reasons:

1. To assure that you are knowledgeable and confident that you CAN qualify

2. To find out exactly how much you can qualify for, and what that monthly payment would look like, so you can include that in the monthly cost equation versus the rent you will take in for any given property.

You will want to know what you are preapproved for, as it is the most important thing to do prior to considering a property to invest in, unless of course, you are purchasing with all cash.

With your finances in place, you know how much the borrowed money will cost you each month, and you will be able to work this into your calculations for more accurate projections when you do the financials for your investment purchase.

With the help of your Realtor, in addition to your own personal online search, you'll be well on your way to looking for and considering properties that are in your comfort range and qualification ability in terms of being doable with your loan and financing. There is no use in looking at properties that you are not interested in or not in your comfort level of affordability, so that's why getting your loan preapproval comes first. You may find an error on your credit report that you will have time to fix upfront, as opposed to being in negotiation on an awesome property, when a fixable error halts progress. It could require a delay in order to remedy, causing you to lose that property to someone else, because you were not well prepared up front. Many people are surprised to find out about errors on their credit report, or unique features to the way they earn income that a lender may need more time and information to process a full qualification. It has the potential to create problems, issues, and delays that you must work out before ever looking at any investment property.

The more property you invest in, the more you will become accustomed to expectations and the procedures for buying and selling investment property, including the local and regional ones customary to the area(s) where you're looking to invest. There are certain standards of practice that change throughout the country, depending on where you are buying. If you are buying out of the area where you currently live, you will definitely be leaning on your Realtor professional to spell out the details and advise you accordingly. You should also be asking a lot of questions as well; remember, be curious and stay informed.

To sum it up, if you believe that you are going to be operating in this market niche, then you will want to follow these steps as guidelines for "buy and hold" investment success:

1. Get fully preapproved for your loan/financing. If possible, get a "DU approval." *

2. Find a Realtor professional and meet to discuss the process, options, potential alternatives, and locations to focus on based on your goals and how much you qualifyfor.

3. Begin your search.

4. Analyze subjectively and objectively the property that hits most or all of your investment criteria—also develop and discuss the investments' exit strategy—are you holding this for a specific amount of time with plans to sell and buy up (more units) or are you holding on to this place for the foreseeable future?

5. Make offer(s) on properties that meet your criteria.

6. An offer eventually gets accepted and escrow begins/opens.

7. Inspections, due diligence, review of reports, leases, financials, more homework, subsequent inspections, etc. will be needed to ensure that the place checks out OK.

8. Interview current property manager (if any) and other potential property managers—decide who will be managing the property if you won't be the active property manager.

9. Finalize financing, insurance, escrow information, and any remainin disclosures and reports.

10. Close escrow.

11. Begin marketing for rental, clean/fix up property.

12. Rent out the property.

13. Manage the property. Eventual implementation of exit strategy.

*DU stands for "Desktop Underwriting."

DU approval is the preeminent automated underwriting system that most all lenders use to preapprove borrowers under the guidelines purveyed by Fannie Mae & Freddy Mac. Because these giant entities buy up and therefore guarantee nearly every mortgage in the U.S., lenders want their loans to conform to these standards and guidelines, so the loan is inherently sellable, hence a "conforming" loan. Getting the DU approval is a notch better than any preapproval you can get, because it's run through the system up-front. Make sure your lender provides this to you if possible, especially when presenting an offer, so the listing agent on the sell side can know you're well approved, fully qualified, and prepared.[9]

Most mistakes are made when you're too optimistic; if you don't calculate conservatively enough on the expenses of the subject propertyorwhen you do not consider what it will take to bring the property to a rentable condition. Follow these above steps, and keep in mind the concepts we have discussed, such as the IDEAL guidelines, for your investment property. Doing so will help you make a sound investment decision and builds confidence to move forward with what will be a solid investment property.

---

[9] http://goo.gl/zkxu89 - Desktop Underwriter Overview: Supporting the origination and underwriting process – 3/19/13

Fix and Flip

The fix and flip investment model is not for the faint of heart. This strategy assumes a lot of risk and speculation. When the market was booming in the mid-2000s, do you remember how many "flipping" TV shows there were on HGTV? It seemed that everywhere in the country, there were people making investments and flipping the houses while cashing out for large sums of money. How many flipping shows do you see nowadays comparatively? There were nearly three dozen flipping shows at the height of the market, and that number went down to zero at the depths of our correction.

But certainly, as the market continues to recover, we will see them becoming popular once more.

Overall, the fix and flip investment model is much more intensive and inherently riskier. More risk implies more reward, but it requires more time and money allocated in order to become successful at this model. The more time you put into your work, the more you will find that your assumptions are more accurate. The more accurate your assumptions, the closer you will get to the actual expected profit on your investment. Sloppy projections, assumptions, and half-assed approaches to this type of investment strategy have ruined many investors, financially. It's high stakes. For the increase in risk, there is certainly increased rewards and return on the initial investment. However, this investment is fickle and can be affected severely by increases and swings in costs of construction, labor, materials, and by market fluctuations.

With the buy and hold strategy, you are in the investment for the long-term. Even if you didn't purchase at the best time, the long-term nature of the investment will help correct an inopportune or untimely purchase. We all see that real estate has gone up and up over time, so the longer you hold the property, the less important the purchase price actually becomes.

This is not true however for "fix and flip" investors. The buy-in price effectively establishes the potential profit. So, many of the best investors (with stocks, real estate, etc.), live by the saying, "You make your profit on the buy-in." In other words, if you cannot purchase the investment property at the most optimal price, you don't give yourself the best opportunity to make the intended profit margin. Many times, an over-optimistic investor goes through with a purchase even though it's at a higher purchase price than they would otherwise prefer, just so they can have a deal or do *something*. As a result, their profit margin is eaten up the minute an unexpected problem or issue is found within the subject property that they are looking to flip. Up to this point, we have only identified the risks of the fix and flip investment strategy and have not even begun to talk about the specifics to make this a winning strategy, which we will discuss in a later chapter. Nevertheless, the more homes you look at, the better you can understand the labor and material costs. You will build better relationships with the vendors and service people that will help in fixing up the property, to get it ready to flip. In addition, you will be more experienced when it comes time to get the heavy lifting accomplished to make your ugly duckling into a beautiful swan of a home, that sells for above list price in a handful of days with multiple offers.

Ideally, the prospect of fixing and flipping would appeal to everyone, because it looks easy from the outside. But it rarely is. It's easy to get caught up in the glamor of what we see on TV or what we think we know. Personally, I wanted to be an architect as I completed college and went to get my Master of Architecture. I wanted this to be my profession, but I was naïve, focusing on the prestige and the benefits of what being an architect could be like, without correctly taking into account the time involved and the opportunity costs in doing so. I was distracted by the glamour of the profession, believing that it wouldn't be difficult to become a successful architect working on extravagant projects and getting paid very well. The reality of the profession really took the wind out of my sails, to say the least. After going through the process, I found that pay would be low—so low that I'd be making less than the high-school kid's earned at the local In-N-Out Burger—with my first position out of graduate school. To make matters worse, acknowledgement, appreciation, and recognition of my work would be scant if any. Before I even finished the first year of the Master's degree program, I wanted out! I was glad that I made the decision to go into business for myself as a professional Realtor, as it got me where I am today. In the same capacity, what happened to me with architecture school can happen to a novice real estate investor attempting to do a fix and flip. Without doing the best you can on your upfront work, by asking questions and getting the most information to make an informed decision, you'll likely get into a sticky situation that you may regret later.

My best advice for the fix and flip: There are medium to large-scale companies, teams of a dozen to several dozen people that are in the business of flipping homes in nearly every city in the country. Rather than entering a market on your own, where companies such as these become your immediate competition, it would be wise to join one of those companies and learn on the job with a team that's already doing several flips a month. This is a great way to gain insight about the trials and tribulations of being a real estate flipper/investor. Consider being an apprentice and doing the grunt work to learn in an immersion program. You will see what works and what doesn't, even if the pay is little or none. The experience drawn from an opportunity like this (assuming you can find it), would be well worth your time invested and with none of the risk compared to learning on your own. This is what I would do if I wanted a fast track to success in the investment real estate game, although, it is easier said than done.

The next best advice is to create an equation that effectively shows the highest allowable offer to make on a home. Then you will know if the current asking price is acceptable or not and your margin (costs), that way you will be less likely to lose money. This is as easy as creating a spreadsheet and taking into account the assumptions of the purchase price, intended fix-up cost budget, sales costs, and working your way backwards to find out the price you can offer to make a specific profit. This way, you can autopilot the decisions based on whether or not you can make an offer, or go higher in price, if you need to win-out on an available property that has several bids—so long as the offered price remains below your max value. If you stick to the plan without deviation, you will have a better chance at hitting your intended goals. You will be making smart decisions as opposed to getting over-emotional and over-paying for a place, and thereby making it terribly difficult to profit on the ensuing flip sale.

You will most likely have to make many, many bids to get an accepted offer. This is going to create issues for you and your agent because you may get discouraged, and your Realtor may not want to continue writing "lowball" bids for you. A well-known flipping company that I have developed a relationship with gave me an account of their success ratio. In a given week, they make about 100 offers on various properties, and out of these 100 offers, they get around a 5% response rate—meaning that 95% of the offers they make don't even get a response. Out of the remaining 5%, they can get an acceptance on one or two of the properties. That's a lot of work and commitment, and that's why some investors get tired of making offers without any luck. Then, they make a rash decision and overspend on a property just to get a property under contract. Nothing is worse than overpaying for a property that you must take a loss on because you can't sell it for a profit.

Lastly, if you couldn't tell already, fix and flip style of investing requires a full-time approach to the subject. Given the time requirements on research, financial analysis, and the oversight of the remodel and sale process, it's nearly impossible to do this in your spare time; it can very easily consume all your time and attention, especially if hardships are experienced along the way. Furthermore, consider your competition; as I mentioned above, there are teams of people in your marketplace that are doing their version of the fix and flip method every single day and getting very good at it. It's not impossible to win on your own, but it's very, very hard. The competition is daunting and it's difficult to break into this market niche. That's why I suggest trying the apprenticeship route as an efficient way to learn the business without taking a risk and spending the money that a flipping business investment strategy will demand. No matter what, this may be the most cut-throat, high-stakes style of real estate investment, precisely because the potential to fail is so much larger than that of the other investment methods mentioned in this book. For someone looking to do this as their investment niche, my best advice is to ensure having sufficient time and resources available, so it will not take away from their day job. If this is going to be a day job, the resources on hand should be sufficient enough to supplement income during the time that you are finding property, and remodeling to flip and sell before you can find or start on the next one.

Tax Shelter

Investment property can be used as a fantastic tax shelter because of the ability to depreciate the property (this was the "D" in the IDEAL guidelines of Chapter 1). The IRS allows you to get a credit for the depreciation of your investment real estate each year, and many investors use this strategy to pay less in taxes. [10] The same way that your car loses value each year, so does the actual building structure on your investment property. The IRS lets you "depreciate" that value and there is a specific process in determining what that value is. However, unlike the car example, under the investment property structure itself is the real estate (land) that you own as well. That, in theory, should be appreciating and this is why the IRS doesn't let you depreciate land. When you are a homeowner getting a tax bill, the tax assessor will typically break out exactly how it came to the final amount of property taxes that you owe. They do this by allocating a value for the structure on the land, as well as the value of the land itself. A good example of this is a client who understands the value in real estate investment, but was also looking to utilize depreciation to the best extent possible. We helped him buy two 4-on-1 properties (4 units on the same piece of property) in the San Diego area, and each of these investment properties were netting him about $2,000 a month. After all expenses, he was realizing an income of about $12,000 annually for each property. Normally, he would have to pay taxes on this income as well as the rest of his ordinary income from

10   http://www.irs.gov/publications/p527/ch02.html - Depreciation of Rental Property

his occupation. However, his depreciation amount for each property is slightly more than $15,000. This means he actually shows a $3,000 loss on the tax returns for each of these investment properties, due to the depreciation of the real estate itself, and he allocates a $6,000 depreciation credit towards the taxes owed on his ordinary income. Therefore, the personal taxes he would otherwise pay are now $6,000 less, and he has no taxes owed on the income of his investment property income. Basically, he is showing a loss even though he is making a profit, due in part to depreciation of the actual home itself. Less money to the IRS means more money in your pocket at the end of each year.

However, the depreciation benefit is not a free lunch. When you go to sell the property, to establish the taxes you owe on profits made from the sale, your accountant (and the IRS) will be expecting to see a line item for "depreciation recapture." Which means what? Every year you are depreciating the house, what does it do to your taxes? They go down, right? But if you think you got a totally free ride, think again. What you were saving on depreciation year after year accumulates and comes back to you when you sell the property. All that nice depreciation has to be added back to your capital gain and increases the taxes you'll owe.[11] (Please refer to our section later in the book on the 1031 exchange so you can avoid these taxes as best as possible.)

Quick Note: I am not a CPA or lawyer—anything tax or legal related in this book is surface level stuff at best for articulation purposes and not intended to be construed as tax or legal advice. You're encouraged to consult and involve your tax and legal professionals when you purchase, so you are kept informed of all the benefits available to you, while also making sure you are protecting yourself to the best extent that is appropriate for your situation.

---

[11] http://www.michaelplaks.com/free-irs-tax-advice/articles-irs-real-estate-tax/irs-depreciation-recapture

Depreciation is a great benefit of investment property ownership. The depreciation amounts get crazy big for larger properties and for high net worth individuals, which makes sense because they will need to purchase a proportionally larger investment property to make a bigger dent in the overall taxes owed for a given year. It's a great thing that I hope you get to experience first-hand very soon!

Mortgage Reduction (Live and Rent Out)

I've worked with many first time homebuyers. Often times, they have the idea that a single family home is the ideal property for them. They never considered or were never offered the option to purchase a duplex, triplex, or 4-on-1 as their first home purchase. Many never considered it because they have the single family home as the main vision in their mind. They want nothing more than to recreate that vision as close as possible. Others don't want to jump into the first time homeowner and landlord shoes all at once. However, as an investment, it's a tremendous idea with potential, if you are comfortable with living very close to the people you are renting to. You need to be tough, yet fair, and by doing so, you can live in a subsidized environment where your tenants are paying for a majority of your mortgage. We have a couple that we have been working with to help them find their first home and their price point is $650,000 (Remember, we're doing business in southern California). They could purchase a duplex for around the same amount. Instead of taking on the entire mortgage payment themselves, by renting out the second unit, they could subsidize their mortgage payment by a substantial degree—to the tune of 30% or more of the mortgage amount. Essentially, the payment is 2/3 of what it normally would be. However, you do make sacrifices in the amount of space and privacy that you may otherwise get with a single family home, as well as having the responsibilities of a landlord. I've met several people who have become independently wealthy as a result of starting their investing career in a manner in which most people don't wish or prefer to do. There are substantial tax benefits to living in and renting out your investment property. In addition, the property is kept in great condition because not only are you living there, but also, I've found that renters will take more care in their use of the property knowing the owner is always close by. Perhaps being a homeowner and landlord simultaneously has some merit for you to consider for your next investment. No matter what, as we have seen continuously, the landlord always ends up on top.

Real Estate Investment as a Hedge on Inflation

Just as there are investors looking for a tax shelter—some investors are looking to invest in real estate specifically with the idea of making the investment a hedge on inflation. It's plausible that within the near future our low interest rate environment will end, as the growth in our economy begins to pick up, which should cause inflation to rise. When it comes to inflation, it's great to be a home-owner (or asset-owner) and not advantageous to be the holder of a loan or have investments in finances, and here's why. As inflation increases, the dollar is worth less. The amount you can buy with your dollar becomes less and less and as a result, stuff becomes more expensive. A home is part of that "stuff" category. Just as the price for a movie ticket or a gallon of milk increases with inflation, so does the cost of housing. It's all relative, however. Let's say that inflation rises 3% this year. For a gallon of milk, it may mean the price increases by a few cents. But for a home, this could translate into thousands upon thousands of dollars. All the while, because of inflation, the actual value of the money for the loan you took out for the purchase of the home is becoming increasingly less. This makes it theoretically easier to pay off, because the value of the dollar is diminishing given the inflation within our economy. A day's work will pay off a higher relative chunk of money from the loan than it did before. This benefits all real estate landlords, owners, and investors, whether they were looking for an inflation hedge or not. It's an excellent benefit of real estate ownership in general, one of the primary reasons that will continue to push real estate values higher in value over time. One thing is certain, moving forward there is less and less "earth" becoming available. Our economic system of capitalism is systemically producing a consistent level of inflation throughout our economy, in which both serve as a boon to homeowners and landlords alike. Therefore, if you're fearful of inflation in the coming future, purchasing investment property may well be the most logical approach to take advantage of what is likely the next most talked-about issue facing the recovery of our nation's economy.

CHAPTER 4

What to buy?

"One thing I tell everyone is learn about real estate.
Repeat after me: real estate provides the highest returns,
the greatest values, and the least risk."

- Armstrong Williams

Single family home or condo?

I N MOST INSTANCES, FIRST TIME REAL ESTATE INVESTORS WILL PURCHASE A home or condo as their investment of choice. This makes sense because this is what they know and are familiar with. As the amount of units you own increase in number and overall value, your experience and desire for bigger and better real estate investments will too. It's typical to begin branching away from the single family home or condo as the investment of choice—put simply, more units under one roof or on one property is more efficient. However, it's possible that you may not have a desire to own a ton of property, and a single family residence may be the perfect fit. It's easy to see why: you know about how much it should cost to run (expenses) from personal experience, and there's only one tenant that you need to manage. In the world of real estate investments, aside from raw land, this is the easiest form of investment, in terms of your time and attention. For condos, you will want to be aware of the Home Owners Association—or HOA for short, and sometimes referred to as common area maintenance fees. Many times in newer subdivisions of single family homes there will be HOA's as well. Keep an eye out for these—not just the overall cost they require each month, but how well run they are. During your transaction, you will want to be able to review the HOA documents, ensure the complex allows for rentals (sometimes they don't or have rental restrictions), be sure the HOA financials are in good health with sufficient "reserves," and that the HOA board is not running the complex into the ground. You will want to take the time to ask people that live in the complex or community about the HOA itself and how they think of it personally. They are the best source for information and they will always give you the most accurate impression of what to expect from the HOA, which is priceless information that can sometimes turn a "buy" into a "pass"—a dodged bullet for sure.

> Quick Story: We once had a client who bought a condo in a complex of about eight units, with the intention to rent that unit out. He realized the building's recycle bin was right in front of his unit. He brought it up with the HOA after we closed, to appeal to change the location. Repeated attempts were made to suggest a different location for the recycle bin, yet the HOA board remained staunchly inflexible; sometimes even the littlest things become a bigger issue when the egos get involved through common community ownership. It can get ugly quick, and although our client wasn't remorseful of his decision to purchase, this is a good example of the minutiae that can become an issue when you purchase investment property. Since then, this same client has purchased two more units in that particular condo complex. I believe his goal is eventually to purchase all the units in the complex so that he can put the recycle bin wherever the heck he wants! However, the point is when you buy into a condo complex, you don't have full control, and sometimes that loss of control can come at a cost. In this case, tenants may not want to rent out a place where the bin is right in front of the unit all the time.

Multi Family or 2-4 units:

Multi-Family or 2-4 units are the next step up from a single family home or condo investment property. The reason I say 2-4 unit specifically is because in California, anything 4 units or below is considered residential property (as opposed to commercial). Once you try to buy a place that has five units or more, then you are in the commercial realm and in need of commercial financing. You are subject to different contracts, policies, procedures, guidelines, and expectations that differ from your typical residential real estate transaction. My personal choice would be 2-4 units, if I could be a first time home investor all over again. My first investment was a single family home because it was an affordable decision—if I could have purchased more units, I would have. The reason why more is better is because of the vacancy factor and for "highest and best use" of my real estate investment. In real estate, with any property you own, you are always looking for the property that makes the "highest and best use of the land". If you have rental property that is a single family home, and the tenant moves out, 100% of your property is now vacant. You then need to fill that vacancy ASAP or else you need to fund and pay for the entire mortgage on your own until you find another suitable tenant. Same scenario, but in a 4-on-1 where you have 4 units on 1 piece of land, and your vacancy only goes to 25% if one tenant moves out. The pinch, if you cannot find a suitable tenant by the month's end, is not nearly as bad. Of course, these properties tend to cost more, which is another reason why the single-family route is so common. Nevertheless, the more units you can control on the same plot of land, the better. I would much rather have 4 "doors" in a single 4-on-1 property as opposed to 4 single family homes. There are less bills to pay, including having one mortgage instead of four. The costs of maintenance are all localized and therefore less in general, and its all-around a more efficient process. Because this is a more efficient use of the land, that is what we refer to as "highest and best use." This is a great way to get you on a solid path for your investment real estate career. If you can swing something like this for your first investment, it'll be easier than you may think.

The following is a quick note on how lenders qualify you for an investment loan. Remember, an investment property is a cash machine and the lender sees it this way. If an investment property is making an income, then the lender will use this income for your benefit when it comes to qualification, with a few conditions. Lenders take 75% of the income (so they can remain conservative) towards your qualification. If a property you wish to purchase has an income of $1,000, then the lender will take $750 towards your qualification. If the mortgage for that property is $750, then the property qualifies *itself.* In this instance, you technically wouldn't need to be making an income and only need good credit along with a down payment to qualify. This is a dreamy example, but you get the picture right? Even if the payment for the property in the above example were $1,250, (a negative cash flow of $250 per month) you would have to qualify for a $500 per month payment ($1,250 less the income the property makes at $750). Most people's car payments are more than $500 a month and that's why it may be easier to qualify for owning investment real estate than one would expect, assuming you have the credit and down payment in place. Follow up with what we reviewed in Chapter 3 in the Buy and Hold section. Speak with your lender soon, before taking major action on your search.

Apartment Building:

The next level up from the 2-4 unit/multifamily property is the apartment building. This can go from five units to 500+ units all on one property. Management starts to become a necessity at this stage. A mentor of mine always told me, "Property management is your friend." You can save money by managing the property yourself, but you also take in all the heartache and any late night emergency calls, which are never fun. Although it differs from state to state, once you get to a certain amount of units, you will be required to have an on-site manager for the tenants in the building. When looking for this type of investment property, this is a very expensive cost and definitely should be taken into consideration in terms of expenses.

Quick Note: In California, a manager is required to be present on the property for any property with sixteen units or more—so if you were adamant on not having a management expense; you would look at everything that was fifteen units or less.

Overall, apartment buildings work and act like bigger and larger 2-4 unit properties. There is usually more opportunity for upside because of the larger amount of units and increased leverage all around.

Strip Mall / Commercial:

Ideally, if you could, you would start here for your first investment, but before we get on the big bike, we need to take some time to get used to the training wheels. Plus, these types of investments are super expensive, making them available for only the more wealthy and/or experienced real estate investors. For many real estate investors, the first investment needs to be a small bite that has a certain level of risk that doesn't "bet the farm." Except in more rural-type areas, strip malls or commercial properties do run substantially more in price as opposed to some of the other investment property types that have been explained already. Commercial and/or strip mall investment real estate generally offers better quality tenants and stronger leases, in favor of the landlord. This is because your tenants are businesses; they are business owners that you are leasing out to as opposed to a random person or family. As a result, your tenants are more long-term in nature and have a vested interest in the betterment of the property, as they want to see their business grow as well. Many times, tenants will spend thousands of dollars for tenant improvements (TI) to furnish their newly leased space in accordance to the business they are trying to operate (i.e., salon, restaurant, financial services, masseuse, etc.). This is the next level for real estate investors or landlords, but the question is, do you have what it takes? This type of investment assumes that you know what you are doing in terms of the leasing, running, and managing a strip mall or commercial property. Unless you already know what you are doing or have the ability to ensure a steep learning curve for the process, this type of investment may not be best suited for your first time real estate investor, but rather as your *next* investment; perhaps you will work your way into this, as it's certainly a higher grade investment overall.

Intensive Commercial:

None of these options are really suited well for the first time investor and are truly outside the scope of this book: industrial, chemical, large retail, office, and all else within the commercial category. They are too-niche to address, given that these investment types probably won't be the properties you will be considering for your first time investment. However, this is a book about investment, so I do wish to address this; but also focus you where you would most likely succeed. Unless you have a massive financial backing to begin with, or have grown up in one of these or related industries, this is not necessarily the best route for you just yet.

Raw Land:

In most cases, the only way raw land makes sense would be with a very long-term investment. You will also want to buy in cash only. If you mortgage a land investment, you are unable to generate an income. Therefore, no cash flow means a substantial loss each month. Even if owned free and clear, you will still be paying property taxes and maybe even an HOA or insurance depending on the lot or piece of land. Enterprising investors are able to flip a lot in very specific instances. One example is, if you know something the seller doesn't. For instance, if you know a piece of land is able to be rezoned or subdivided to resell for a profit, it may be worth the risk to make that investment. However, this is a rare instance. For the most part, land investment requires it to be a long-term play, so be ready for that.

Quick Story: A close associate of mine purchased a small parcel of land in Florida about twenty years back. At the time, it was worth $20,000. He thought he was a fool when prices dipped down after a recession that followed shortly after the purchase. He would have been lucky if he could sell that plot of land for $2,000 at the bottom of that particular market cycle. Nevertheless, he kept the land, and five years went by. He started getting notices in the mail from investors offering $20,000 for his parcel. Although he would finally be able to sell it for what he paid, he decided to continue owning the plot and not responding to any solicitations. Well, the market continued to improve, and another year or so went by and offers for $30,000 were being made by local investors looking for available land to develop. The next year, the offers increased to the $40,000 range. This trend continued into the peak years of the market cycle and he ended up selling that plot of land for $120,000. Interestingly enough, because of the correction in the market following that peak from which he sold, you could purchase the same plot for about $20,000. Within a fifteen-year period, this same plot of land was valued at $2,000 at the low end and $120,000 at the absolute peak—how crazy is that? But that's Florida real estate for you!

With land, you really play off the potential or expected future opportunity at hand. This will be the main determining factor in the investor's mind that will be purchasing land from you (hopefully, for profit) in the future.

A Few Words About Timeshares . . .

Timeshares? My advice is that you NEVER buy one. I don't advise this or recognize it as an investment vehicle of any sort. A timeshare is a money vacuum, where it's your money and someone else's vacuum. Under most circumstances, you should stay away because there is no market to sell your timeshare back; and through the purchase, you marry yourself to a specific location, or a brand, or both. This is the worst type of a real estate "investment" you can involve yourself with (if you want to call it an investment at all). It's a complete waste of time and money, and only in the most specific of circumstances can a timeshare be beneficial—if you actually like the place and use it each year, religiously, and in bliss—but for 99% of the people out there, it's not.

Hotels, vacation ownership companies, and timeshare companies spend a bunch of cash and train sales people to give you the most compelling prospects and reasoning of why you should "invest" in a timeshare. They sell a dream. They will wine and dine, offering gifts and cash incentives; they will offer points and trade-off programs for the weeks that you cannot make the trip. They show you how much money you can save. All of it is 100% BS, in my opinion.

Word of advice: If the benefits are too good to ignore and you must go to their "pitch," just get the free stuff but leave your credit card and check book at home.

A timeshare is essentially a $1/52^{nd}$ lifetime lease of a property. That is a week out of a year for you. However, to the developer and owner of a timeshare, they are able to lease a property out fifty-two times over with stiff regulations, penalties, and maintenance fees. In the case of the timeshare, you're not the landlord. Therefore, you're more than likely being taken advantage of, so beware of the timeshare.

Just imagine you bought a timeshare and now you want to try to sell it. You'd never be able to match the same marketing dollars that are being spent luring people into those timeshare presentations and seminars—that's your competition. Outside of these timeshare seminars, there's nobody looking to buy a timeshare, and that's why it takes so much intentional finesse, incentive, and highly persuasive presentation technique to get people to buy these things in the first place.

"Hey can I buy your timeshare from you?"—said nobody ever.

This is the biggest drawback. Nobody wants to buy the timeshare from you if you want to sell. If you don't have any legitimate buyers, then your timeshare is essentially *worthless*. It's not an investment at all, so by all means, stay away.

You'd think from this passage that I'm a bitter owner of a timeshare, but I'm not. I've never bought one. However, I've seen enough people complain and lament about their timeshare woes to know better. No matter what, that shouldn't be you. Please, vacation at will instead of being stuck in Puerto Vallarta for the rest of your life for week twenty-three—and no, I don't care that you can trade points. You are being played by the game if you think points are the answer. No timeshare, not an investment. No. Class dismissed.

Tax Liens, Other, etc.

Anything else I haven't covered as of yet is too-niche and specific for singular coverage in the book. If there is a niche and it's worthwhile after doing your research and homework, it may pay to become the local go-to professional investor for that specific niche. Because our country is so vast, there are several niche areas and specialties, such as tax liens or tax certificates, which an investor can get involved with. Do your due diligence to be sure the property types we have already covered would not work for you before branching off and blazing your own trail. I never try to stifle creativity or say no to new opportunity, but sometimes it's better to not reinvent the wheel. For hundreds of years, many people have become successful and wealthy with the above methods. As a result, it may be easier to go with the familiar at first, before using an exotic approach to real estate investment.

CHAPTER 5

When to buy?

"I always felt very secure and very safe with real estate. Real estate always appreciates."

- Ivana Trump

I
F YOU ARE READING THIS BOOK, THEN THERE'S A GOOD CHANCE YOU ARE going to be purchasing an investment property in the near future, but how do you know if it's a good time to buy and when you should pull the trigger? Most real estate agents will never say it's not a good time to buy, because for real estate agents, it's ALWAYS a good time to buy. With all seriousness, trying to game the market to time your purchase as best as possible is not a winning strategy. Whether its stocks or real estate, nobody can accurately time a market peak or market trough. We only know we hit the high or the low well after it already happened—in most cases, it's six months following. Therefore, instead of looking outward at the market and searching for the signs on when exactly to purchase, it's much more effective and efficient to determine when it is the best time for you personally to make that investment purchase.

Learn:

Nothing beats real world experience. With real estate investing, you'd be best to learn from other people's mistakes rather than learning from your own. Not only is it costly, ruinous, and time-consuming to go through the process of a bad real estate investment, it may put a sour taste in your mouth for real estate investing in general. Sloppy homework, rash decisions, poor analysis, and execution equate to the kiss of death and welcome a poorly performing investment property. Real estate investing is not an easy thing to do, and if it was, everyone would do it. We know that landlords have historically been the world's most wealthy class of private citizens, so it literally pays to learn it. Live it and thrive from the fruits of the effort you have put in.

With the fundamentals in hand,, youre encouraged to go to work by beginning the process of researching for the property type of choice.

Research:

Research has two fronts. One is the research for your financing, and the other is research on the property type that you are searching for to become your real estate investment.

For your financing, you want to be fully pre-approved and vetted for the loan you are looking to acquire as a part of your purchase. It doesn't matter when you want to buy if you cannot get a loan to secure your purchase. We covered the steps for this in the Buy and Hold section of Chapter 3, regarding financing. While you get pre-approved, make sure the loan officer you are working with is offering the best "fit" in terms of the type of loan you are trying to get, in addition to the best rate. For example, if you are looking to purchase an investment and hold it for no more than five years, then your loan officer may suggest a five year Adjustable Rate Mortgage (ARM), instead of a thirty year fixed-rate mortgage. Typically, the ARM's interest rate is lower and can save you a lot of money over the five-year period as well as increasing your monthly cash flow—just have a potential back up plan in the event you cannot sell in five years or decide to do otherwise. When you are fully approved and are confident with the rate and terms, you can move forward in earnest with regards to making offers on the property type you are looking to purchase.

Note: Most investment property loans require a minimum of 20% down, and in some cases, as much as 30% down in order to qualify for a loan. There are alternatives. In Chapter 3, we discussed the idea of "live and rent," whereby you are living in the multi-unit investment property you have purchased and are renting the others out. In this case, you are able to secure residential, owner occupied loan programs; one of which is an FHA product that can allow you to purchase a property with as low as 3.5% down payment—a far cry from 30% down. It can get confusing and technical very quick when it comes to financing. Therefore, find a great loan officer to work with sooner rather than later, especially before going headstrong into the search process. If you don't have a great lender to work with, check the back of the book for the resource section, and we can refer a great lender for you and your prequalification.

Research on the property begins with isolating the property type and/ or niche you are looking to focus on. We covered the different strategies of investment (such as fix and flip or buy and hold) earlier in Chapter 3 as well as the types of property that investors will typically invest in, in Chapter 4. When you have narrowed down the strategy and property type by weighing the positives and negatives against your current situation, available funds, and investment goals in mind, you can then have a specific kind of property type in focus with the exit strategy to go with you throughout the analysis part of your purchase.

For example, suppose I am a beginner investor with somewhat limited funds for a down payment. I am looking to buy and hold my first investment property with the intention of holding it for the long-term and being able to pay it off to own it free and clear. Because my down payment is limited, I can qualify for a loan amount that allows me to purchase a property for the going rate that a two or three unit investment property sells for in the area I am interested. I'll get in touch with and work hand-in-hand with my Realtor to identify the best properties in the location(s) I want to focus on, as well as getting their input as to any alternatives. They may know of other locations that will work with the same purchase price that I may not have already considered. With the area(s) and price limit in mind, we can put the search together for all two or three unit investment properties (maybe even 4 units if we can find any available under my max price). I'll begin to get the search results and proceed with the analysis process by seeing what returns are being provided by each property, given my down payment and each properties income and expenses. We will cover these specifics of evaluating property later on in the book, but this is the general sequence of steps you will take moving forward.

BONUS - Finding a great Realtor: If you don't have one, how do you find a great Realtor professional to help you with your investment purchase? We've got you covered. At the back of the book, you can find a resource section. As part of the benefit of purchasing this book, you can have access to my Realtor database of great professionals throughout the country. Over the years, we've assembled a great network of agents from all over that work the same way we do and can help you get to where you want to be. We can source a solid professional for you to help you get where you are looking to be, faster.

Visit the property:

The drive by—when you get the search results from your own search or the custom search that your Realtor has put together, you should begin driving through the areas of the subject properties. Driving by will help you discover whether the surrounding area of the subject property is worth investing in. Run-down or rough areas will attract a similar type of tenants, all things being equal. The best and most prestigious areas of town will attract only the type of person that can afford the higher rent.

> Quick Note: When you drive by the investment property itself, do the "MOM" test. More specifically, the "MOM" test means if you would feel uneasy about sending you own mother to that area to collect a rent check at night, then you may wish to pass on that property. Surely the only reason you are clinging to the possibility of the property is due to the low, attractive price. Just remember: bad property equals bad tenants, and bad tenants usually equates to a bad property.

It's wise to pay more for a better property, which will attract better tenants. This inherently improves the ability for the property to last longer with less maintenance issues. Doing the drive by gets you further clued in on the areas that can allow you better insight as to the nuances of the local area you are focusing on. This will help you analyze why some places can command certain rents over others, and will help allow you to eliminate the areas that aren't up to the standards you are looking for. This system works for all kinds of investment property types as well as the different strategies we have discussed. Not only does this work for investment property, it's the process we encourage for all our primary home buyers as well.

Visiting the property is important. I write about it specifically because many times investors purchase property "sight-unseen," meaning they make an offer without actually seeing the property itself. This may be OK for a seasoned investor—one who is well versed with the property type, location, etc. However, for the first-time investor, NEVER purchase a property sight-unseen.

Quick Story: The one investment I personally regret having made was one that was "sight-unseen". Early in my career, I was compelled to purchase a property on the other side of the country in a location that was affordable and attractive. I relied on the salespeople to assist me with the purchase, but in retrospect, they didn't have my best interests in mind. I could have done a better job in the selection process than the agent assisting me. The property we had selected was purchased. A few months later, we visited the property for the first time. I did a decent amount of research upfront, but the area I purchased in was so newly developed that Google maps were not updated to show what the streets looked like. Therefore, when I finally arrived to view the property that I owned in person, I found hundreds, if not thousands of other properties and developments just like it. It seemed the entire area was overbuilt and I purchased right into the peak of price momentum. Had I taken the time and spent the money to visit the property before or even during the purchase process, I would have realized the severe glut of inventory, the obvious problem of being able to re-sell (exit strategy), and the fact that it failed when put to the IDEAL investment property guidelines. Although this was a small investment, the fact that it could have been avoided is what sticks with me, always. Had I visited the property in addition to doing the research, I would have been able to dodge the bullet. Now, I am stuck with a property that will take a lot longer to sell than I was initially expecting. This is why it's important, especially for your first investment, to physically visit your property and get a feel for the area to make sure the property feels right and will perform with the assumptions that you are working off of before you close escrow. If anything feels funny, it's OK to walk away. A bad investment hurts much more than no investment made in the first place.

This reminds me of another story while going through the rut of the recession. I remember a company that specialized in selling foreclosed property at ludicrously low prices throughout the country. This company worked with major banks and purchased entire portfolios of foreclosed homes, which allowed them to purchase many homes at once for pennies on the dollar. The issue at hand was that the homes they were taking over were in the slummiest areas of the country. They were hit the hardest through the downturn of the recession. The attractiveness of the homes they were selling was the price; you could purchase a single family home from this company for about $10,000, with the possibility of cash flow being several hundred dollars each month. If you did a drive by and vis-ited these places, you would realize the home was situated in an area that was massacred with foreclosed properties. Sure, you could purchase and own a home for less than the price of a car, but you would be more likely to find someone squatting in your home than you could find someone actually willing to pay rent. This home investment would fail in the IDE-AL guideline test that we talked about in Chapter 1. Although cash flow was the lure that got your attention, the ability to rent would be slim and difficult, and the upside appreciation on home was substantially limited. This strategy worked for the short-term, but the realities of the underly-ing problems of the investment inevitably led to failure of the company offering the properties. Properties that did get rented out had the ten-ants stop paying, or major rehab issues came up within months of the purchase. Most investors were savvy enough to know a bad investment when they saw one. Even for the novice beginning investor, if they were lucky and smart enough to do a drive by and visit the property they were considering to purchase, they would have avoided a major headache. Not every investment opportunity is a great opportunity just because the price is low.

More research:

By refining your criteria and focusing on location, there will only be a few properties that match the best. Once you've done your research, it will soon be easy to spot the best deal available on the market. From this point on, as long as it's in the desired area and makes the expected return on investment (or fits the specific needs of the real estate investor), it would be an appropriate time to make a bid/offer on the best property (or properties).

Many times, with multi-family property or anything larger than a single unit, the showing instructions may state that they are, "shown with accepted offer." Although it may sound funny, most buyers will make a bid on a property with only seeing the outside first, and then digging deeper once the offer is presented, negotiated, and accepted. If the listing agent showed every buyer that was interested the inside of the unit(s), it's easy to see that the tenant(s) would be inconvenienced by the multitude of showings. Then they may leave the property before the sale ended, and nobody wants to inherit a property that is already vacant, when through a more refined means of showing the home, it wouldn't have otherwise happened. That said, this is the reason that most investment property is "shown with accepted offer" only.

When you are viewing places it's important to remain neutral. This will NOT become your home. This is an investment property that renters will be looking to rent. With that in mind, we should remain objective when viewing potential properties and ensure the rents stated are actual rents that can be sustainable. At this point in time, you've presented your offer, negotiated back and forth, and with some luck, have an offer that gets accepted. Once this happens, you will open up escrow and you will have begun your "due diligence" period on the property to determine that it is in a current condition that is acceptable to move forward with the deal. If the inspection highlights issues of concern with the property, you can confer with your agent to discuss a request for a credit or repair, and determine if a credit through escrow is appropriate for negotiating with the seller or if the seller can oversee repairs prior to closing.

Note: Buyers have the right to ask, but sellers are not obligated to agree or respond to these requests. Although it depends on the market, I'd like to say that sellers generally will accommodate buyer repair/credit requests in order to keep the deal together, assuming the original request by the buyer was a fair one.

We will move forward with the assumption that this is the best property in question. It made the short list from your initial research. If all checks out and this property is in a good enough condition to move forward, we make our way towards the close of escrow.

What's the backup plan if plan A doesn't work? Always have a backup plan in place—just in case! Remember from earlier, the strongest card a buyer usually holds in the negotiation process is the ability to back out of the contract completely. If something comes up during the due diligence period that is too much to handle or take on, you should have a backup plan in place. Nine times out of ten with our clients, once we have gone through the research phase and indicated the place(s) that are the best opportunities available, and once an offer is made and accepted, that property becomes sold and transfers hands. The exception to this is when we make an offer on the property and find the condition of the property or the leases/rents aren't as expected or advertised. In which case, we would renegotiate terms on price, etc. or back out of the deal entirely.

Make offers and buy:

Some of our most successful investor clients are the ones that make A LOT of offers. If the offer isn't accepted then they move on to the next opportunity and don't think anything of their non-accepted offer. They don't take the rejection personally at all. I file my emails in Microsoft Outlook, and one investor client of ours has by far the most files because he has made the most offers. When I review the places that he has actually bought, I found that he has essentially secured and purchased the least expensive deals that we have ever been a part of. In other words, he has been able to buy several investment properties for much less than anyone else because he is present, persistent, and has a specific bottom line in mind. The more offers you write, the more chances you get to own property. Because of the price point we were at for this client, it made sense to write a lot of offers. This may not be the case for you specifically; however, the underlying logic remains clear and true. You should make offers and feel confident in doing so to better ensure a successful purchase process. That is assuming that the underlying property makes sense in terms of price, location, and style/condition.

If you feel ready, and the financing is in place, then it's time to buy. Only in the most heated and oversold of real estate markets should you take the outward pressures of the market into consideration. In that event, the market is increasing so much you may wish to remain on the sidelines. With where we stand today, it's my personal belief that we will be experiencing several years of positive real estate value growth, given the fact that we have just come out of a major recession. Throughout history, real estate values always increase and eventually outpace and exceed the values of the previous highs in the market. We will effectively see new highs being created in this current market cycle. It's my hope that you can get involved and invested in order to realize the appreciation that is expected as a result of our current position in the real estate market cycle overall.

CHAPTER 6

Where to buy?

"There are three things that matter in property: location, location, location."

- Lord Harold Samuel

STRATEGIES ON WHERE TO BUY YOUR INVESTMENT PROPERTY LIE SOLELY with your comfort zone and your budget. If you can't afford to find a place nearby where you currently own, it may be advantageous to buy an investment property in a different state. When it comes down to it, there is no right or wrong answer on where to buy; it just needs to make sense for you personally and financially.

Having your property close by:

I once had a client that owned several investment properties and all of them were within a thirty-minute drive from his home. He had more of an old-school mentality. He was a seasoned and well-experienced real estate investor and at the point in his successful career where he was lending money to other investors, essentially becoming the bank for other people in addition to the multitude of properties that he owned. He swore by a thirty-minute rule; he would say that if he couldn't drive to his property and back in time for lunch he wouldn't invest in it. This was a rule that wasn't always in place for him. He would recount earlier in his investment career that he would buy anything and everything that he could get his hands on, and whatever he could get a loan for. This is probably the reason he has been so successful. Although it sounds a bit less conservative than I would otherwise recommend. He's been intentional with goals in mind and has made a lot of offers along with personal investment guidelines, or mantras being created along the way. When he was younger, he was aggressive and willing to go wherever the deal was, but at this stage in life, given his success and what he already owned, he grew to be more conservative and cognizant of what he would pull the trigger on. He appreciated the ability to go see the properties that he owned, and with them only being a short drive away, he had a better sense of control upon them. This was important to him because it was a personal preference that he liked to be close to the assets he owned and managed. Yet, from a more practical perspective, if you can buy a reasonable investment home in the location you live, it is preferable to that of owning property far away. The most obvious reason being that if something goes wrong or runs amok with the property, not only are you close by to handle it, you will/should have a team in place to address the problem or issue head-on. If you wish to improve the property, you can meet at the place and bid out the improvements accordingly. If the place isn't being managed according to your wishes or preferences, you can see for yourself whether or not the property manager is doing a good enough job. You can see if the tenants are taking care of the property or helping to increase the deferred maintenance. By all accounts, it makes good sense to be close by to your investment properties.

Why would someone consider another location other than the area in which they currently live? It will come down to a few basic reasons and concepts.

Out of area Investing:

A desired property may not be available on the market for the price the investor is looking to spend in their local area. I personally own properties outside the state I live in. One happens to be in southern Texas. Why southern Texas? Well, because a single family house would cost $75,000 there, and the same house, if removed and replaced into San Diego (which happens to be my home area), would be $400,000 or more. This was the price point I could afford at the time I wanted to act and when I was ready to make an investment. As such, because nothing around me was available for the price I could afford (wanted) to pay, I had to go outside the state in order to do so. Our Texas place has been a positive cash flow investment from the day we purchased it, and it's retained its value over the past few years, even during the recession where the value of most homes throughout the country have taken a beating. With sound logic going into the investment, I pulled the trigger and it's been a good investment for me personally.

This brings up another reason an investor may opt to go elsewhere for their investment: diversity. If you already own a home in one location and buy an investment in that same location, both properties will be subjected to the ebb and flow of that particular market. If I owned a home in San Diego, and decided to purchase my investment property in south Texas, where the San Diego home went down in value over the past three years, the Texas property remained stable and slightly positive. The same concept rings true for stocks, where you diversify with a blend of differing types of stocks and bonds to help balance out and hedge against major fluctuations in the financial markets. That's what we can do here in real estate as well, and you can also extend this concept to purchase other types of property (commercial, etc.) in an attempt to hedge your real estate holdings. You may wish to go outward a bit.

Lastly, specific opportunity; there may just be an awesome amount of opportunity in a location that is nowhere close to home for you, but you're willing to go for it anyway. Consider Las Vegas. Las Vegas is a market that has been so vastly over-built and over-leveraged that a majority of the homes throughout the city are upside-down. This means that a majority of homes still have mortgages where the owner owes more than the actual property is worth, even this far into the recovery. It's a telltale sign of buying into the peak and subsequent crash of the real estate market. It's a disaster of a market place and as a result the entire town has been swamped with foreclosures and short sales since 2007. Las Vegas felt the correction hard, in fact, maybe the hardest of all metropolitan areas throughout the country based on the intense level of speculation that ramped up prices of properties in the first place. However, since then prices have gone down—way down. You could purchase a home there for as little as $30,000 in the depths of the recession and get a 20% return on investment, but now it's more like $100,000 and less than a 10% return on investment as the rebound is very much in effect and more and more buyers and investors are parking their dollars in Las Vegas. Most of the homes in Las Vegas were mostly all built in the real estate boom; therefore, a majority of the available inventory in Las Vegas is homes that are only a few years old. Investors see the opportunity here. They know that they can purchase a place for less than "the cost of replacement." In other words, it would cost way more to rebuild a similar home with all construction and labor costs, than its current purchase value, which is a rare dynamic to find, but has become more common throughout our recession and correction.

In other words, if it cost $150 a square foot to build a 1,000 square foot home, then the total cost to build this home would be $150,000. Yet, in Las Vegas you can find this home (which is like new—only a few years old) for much less than this cost, which is ridiculously cool for investors. The places rent out because the underlying economy is a strong one (supported by the gambling, tourism, and military sectors), and this is a recipe for a great buy. This is why there is currently no inventory for property anymore in Las Vegas. It's why every listing that comes on the market gets a ton of offers because the savvy investors are seeing these trends and the inherent opportunity. It's why prices have more than tripled since the bottom of the market in many cases. Who wouldn't want to purchase a place that's less than replacement cost and only a few years old (so little, if any, deferred maintenance), and brings in solid rents because there are more renters now than places that are available to rent. Just make sure you do the drive by and visit the property first!

The same thing can be said for parts of Phoenix as well. The demand is such that it is beginning to have a substantially positive impact on prices due to the overall demand. Although opportunities like these may not exist in your local area, these examples may push you to consider going out of town or out of state for your first investment purchase.

> Note: This is the way to think about investment real estate—stay curious and get creative because identifying trends, patterns, and behavior is key. No one way is the right way, and any investment can be a great one for many different reasons. Before you are too caught up in your own hype, pitch your investment idea to an honest neutral party to see if you are on track or way off base.

No matter where you end up purchasing, be sure that it makes sense by running the property through your IDEAL test and that you have seen the place first. (Remember—no "sight-unseen" offers!) After that, it all comes down to preference and budget. Although it's nice to have your property close by, if you do have to go elsewhere there are ways to determine which places are better than others.

Researching Your Area(s) of Interest:

There is a plentitude of data out there for demographic and socio-economic trends relative to real estate and a community in general. For example, a property investor is better off purchasing in Austin or Dallas as opposed to Detroit.[12]

Why? If this was forty years ago, the opposite would be true, but Detroit is a dying city that's trolling through bankruptcy. Its main com-

---

[12]   http://versus.com/en/detroit-vs-austin

petitive advantage for jobs is the auto industry, which has been on a long-term decline for decades now as companies continue to close down and leave the area. Because this area relies heavily on this industry, the jobs that the industry supports will go along with it and so does the income that particular job would offer a person to pay the mortgage, taxes, etc. More so, it has an effect on other local businesses as there is less money to go around for local restaurants, stores, and the like, which make matters worse. People tend to pack up and leave. Nobody is paying taxes. There are very few jobs available as businesses are closing up shop, and little is being maintained on a civic level. Detroit is in the state it's in now due to the lack of economic and employment promise. It has had more net migration out of the area, as opposed to into the city. Contrast that to Austin or Dallas. These Texas cities have become middle of America meccas of the technological industry. Well-paying jobs that come along with the high tech industry can fund the mortgages that pay for the homes, increasing housing demand and boosting prices, along with overall quality of life in the areas that people settle in. Even if I was to get a steal of a deal in Detroit, because of the larger systemic issues in relation to the overall economy, the long-term prospects don't look great for Detroit and the entire area of the country affectionately known as the, "rust belt." We aim for growth and development, and if you get it right, it can pay off handsomely—remember the example of the people who bought a home in San Francisco in the 1960s and1970s? Whether these people knew it or not, the massive growth and development increased the value of a home that was a couple thousand dollars, and it turned into several million. Yes, it took a few decades to get there, but I'll challenge you to find another investment that has the power to do this along with the other benefits that investment real estate offers without insanely increased risk.

If you are considering venturing into a different area or state for your investment property, check out the available data. A research company called Woods and Poole do great demographic research on a level of detail similar to that of the U.S. census. You can see if a given area is gaining population or losing it. You can see what the median income is, age, the major industrial sectors that a given city contains, and so much more. It's good to know this and use the information to your advantage. Then you want to go to the area and check it out for yourself. Is there a lot of stuff for sale? For rent? Are the streets well maintained or is there a lot of graffiti and vagrancy? You will want to check out the level of development. Are all the buildings aging without renovation, or are there new construction projects being put in? You will want to consider the businesses that are in the area as well.

Quick Story: While I was in South Texas looking for investment property to analyze, I saw a Target that was nearing completion (They were installing the big logo on the front of the building). A Home Depot had just opened, and there was an open lot just breaking ground with a big sign showing that it was going to be a future Costco within the next year. I noticed these multi-million dollar companies investing their dollars in the area that I was considering investing in, and I know they have a heck of a lot more money, people, and time to do the research in this area than I did. I was convinced after doing the research and seeing the data in real life by visiting in person. I found the area attractive enough to move forward and consider property. It was a growing area, worthy of my investing into it.

If you live in an area like Detroit, it would be wise to invest in an area other than your hometown as a means to hedge the decline in desirability and growth in your area. Just make sure the area you do invest in has the underpinnings of growth, desirability, and future development. After all, it's all about location, location, location, and this is a surefire way to ensure your property both appreciates in value and (if desired) will have a great chance to find decent tenants all year long.

CHAPTER 7

Why?

"I meet with a lot of successful entrepreneurs, and almost every one of them has taken profits from their businesses over the years to invest in rental property. Based on this fact, I have consistently urged my clients to buy one rental property a year and already have clients with rental properties earning them money they never imagined they'd have. The far majority of us will never get rich overnight. It takes long-term investing and a diverse portfolio to build true wealth. Don't forget real estate as an important part of the equation."

- Mark J. Kohler

So, WHY INVEST IN REAL ESTATE IN THE FIRST PLACE? THERE ARE several reasons and benefits that are outlined throughout this text thus far, but if you were to reduce it down to one word it would be, opportunity. There is just so much potential in a given real estate investment. A buyer of real estate owns a piece of the United States as opposed to some infinitesimal share of ownership in a company when it comes to investing in the stock market. With the exception of starting your own business, owning real estate is perhaps the quintessential American investment, as owning property has deep seeded roots in what we would call the, American Dream. You're not just investing in your future; when you buy a piece of investment property, you are being able to realize an investment that produces monthly income, allows for taxable depreciation, builds wealth (hopefully), and provides shelter for a fellow citizen if you rent it out. It's a noble thing to be a good landlord, and through the centuries it appears that if you are a landlord, you're generally more well-off than the average citizen. Perhaps the right question is, "why not?" instead of "why?" when it comes to owning investment property. If you were to follow the prescribed strategies and tips as outlined thus far in the book, there should be no reason the investment made is not a good one that provides dividends while increasing the net worth of the individual investor.

Digging deeper - The Other Main Reasons One Opts for a Real Estate Investment:

Tangible Property – When you buy real estate, you own a piece of property. It's not an intangible slice of a company that is represented by a number on a computer screen. You pay property taxes that are deductible, and you can depreciate against it as opposed to a financial investment. You hold ownership to a slice of America. Even if it's a blue chip stock that you own, I would always give this country the benefit of the doubt compared to any business within the stock market, no matter how large the underlying company of the stock you own may be. If crap hit the fan and you needed to live in your investment, you could. No other investment vehicle allows for this. Anyone can own stock, and there is nothing wrong with it, as it's important to diversify accordingly, but you couldn't live in your stock, bond, or money market if you needed to. Many people invest with blind hope that things will go well when it comes to equities, because at the end of the day, they don't know what they are doing anyway. Yet, they fund their IRA or 401K and hope for the best. Not everyone has what it takes to be a landlord, but my point is that the ones that do take on this role and responsibility end up winning in the game of life. It may take added risk, time, and effort, but it pays off in the end and is worth it after all is said and done. My best advice is to be the landlord, while funding your retirement, stocks, and bonds. In this way, you are fully diversified to most every asset class. Nevertheless, the tangibility of real estate is a unique appeal that no other asset can really provide.

Illiquid – Have you ever had a stock that was worth one amount at the close and opened the next day and it was drastically more or less than when it closed just hours earlier? That kind of volatility doesn't really exist in the real estate market. It's more tempered because you can't just sell a home with the click of a mouse. You need to have multiple parties, loads of documentation and disclosure, inspections, reports, renegotiations, and financing involved—all of this takes valuable time and nothing is done really quickly. This is good because it tends to keep drastic decisions from being made. Instead of being able to cash out on your home within minutes, it's going to take, in most cases, at least a couple of weeks. Sometimes this can be a hindrance, but it's really nice to have so many checks and balances in place to ensure that buyer and seller are dealing together at a fair market value and that both parties are being represented and served in a professional manner. Sometimes emotions and fears get in the way and a drastic sell or impulse purchase is made with stock and other financial investments—because of the nature of the turnaround times in real estate, nothing is truly impulsive as there is no instant gratification. It's as thought out and intentional as it can be, and it ends up being in the best interests for all sides this way.

Depreciation/Tax Shelter – Investors looking for an investment that will allow them to be able to shelter their taxable income often utilize investment property as a means to do so. We gave an example of this exact concept earlier in the book—in fact, depreciation is one of the main benefits in owning investment real estate in the first place. Essentially, as everyone knows, when you drive a brand new car off the lot, it reduces in value; the same thing applies to the structure on top of a given piece of land. There are standard accounting principles that the IRS allows and accepts for residential and commercial property where they will determine the value of the structure specifically (land cannot be depreciated) and divide by either the commercial or residential depreciation rate. This amount would be the amount you can "depreciate" each year for your tax benefit. Even if you are operating with a cash flow on your property, when you take into account the depreciation amount you may actually show a net loss for the year for the property. For example, if I could cash flow $10,000 a month, and after calculating depreciation, the depreciation amount was $15,000, I would then be able to claim a loss of $5,000 per month and be able to further utilize this loss towards any other taxes I may owe. This is a phenomenal quality of real estate investment property.

Cash Flow and Appreciation – We all want cash flow and lots of appreciation, and they are a no-brainer for why you would want to invest in property in the first place. If it's not going to appreciate, then you are almost better off holding cash and not buying anything. However, sometimes we have clients that wish to sell, even though they will take a loss and are able to effectively take that loss and use it to the best of their ability against any current taxes that are owed. Nonetheless, the primary goal with any investment property (any investment, for that matter) is the appreciation of the underlying asset. Although nothing is guaranteed, if you follow the concepts as stated in this book, you will have fantastic opportunity to realize the success of your real estate goals and invest in a fantastic property that will provide all the benefits outlined in the IDEAL acronym introduced in the beginning of this book. When you purchase with the IDEAL investment guidelines in mind—it's really difficult to mess this up.

Diversification – It's a fact that many Americans have their wealth tied to their home, so much so that in 2012 for the first time ever, the average Canadian's net worth eclipsed that of the average American's net worth.[13] This is mostly because the U.S. experienced nearly seven years of decimated real estate values, whereas Canada's real estate markets have remained stable and strong throughout the "great recession" experienced by the United States. During this same time, many people throughout the U.S. experienced a double whammy of declining real estate values as well as a decline in their investment portfolio. It was a bad time for those that saved and built a fabulous nest egg, just to see nearly half of it disintegrate between 2007 and 2009.

---

[13] http://www.usnews.com/news/articles/2012/07/18/for-the-first-time-canadians-now-richer-than-americans

Although we are back at an all-time high for the stock market, the bottom line is that the key to overall success with any investment is diversification performed consistently over a span of time. And what's a greater way to diversify than by purchasing an investment real estate property and holding it long enough to pay it off? You ought to diversify against the market volatility of your financial investment and retirement accounts with investment real estate. There is no single pathway to success, but the recipe offered here is quite simple. It's confusing that more people don't follow the sage advice that many successful individuals have offered as the pathway to financial freedom, independence, and security.

Tax Deferred Investment (1031 exchanges) – When it comes to investment property, the idea is to operate with a method in which you should never pay taxes on a gain, ever again. More specifically, as you continue to move forward and purchase investment property, you will want to sell, eventually, and then buy again. However, this time the property is a bigger and better investment—and then you'll want to repeat this process several times over, the goal is to not have to pay the tax man at all throughout this process. Here's how: We call this a 1031 "tax deferred" exchange. The 1031 corresponds to the actual tax code from the IRS addressing this topic. Perhaps the problem lies with calling the procedure an exchange, as this creates a lot of misunderstanding, and would be better utilized if this were re-labeled as a 1031 rollover, because that is precisely what happens. In the most basic sense, doing a 1031 exchange will allow you to sell an investment property that you own for profit, and promptly transfer all of that profit into a new investment property within a specified timeframe. By doing it under the terms and conditions the IRS mandates, you don't have to pay taxes on the profit made from your sale until you actually sell the newly purchased place, but there is no limit on the times you can do a 1031 exchange.

The strategy here would be to continuously buy and sell via the 1031 exchange process. For example, turning a duplex into a 4-plex, then from the 4-plex to a 10-unit apartment, and then the apartment complex into a strip mall, and then from the strip mall to a large commercial retail building. All the while, you can withhold and avoid paying the taxes that you would otherwise have had to pay on the profit from each sale. The key here is to buy and maintain the properties as they get bigger and bigger through life. Through retirement, you live off the cash flow, but through the entire process, you've built a considerable net worth that continues to grow, allowing you to have a legacy of wealth to pass down. Then when you do finally go, you've left a fantastic portfolio of investment property in which to bequeath to your extended family, trust, etc., before actually paying the accumulated taxes over the years due to a "stepped-up" tax basis.[14]

Just leave that stuff to your inheritors or your organization. This is a great strategy to create a legacy. There is no singular right way to go about this, but this is the way my wife and I are going about building our worth and legacy.

What's more is that what would otherwise be paid to the IRS from profits made is going straight into your next investment, so you can afford a bigger and better "step up" investment property throughout the process. It's a wonderful thing that not a lot of people know about, but if you are planning on investing in real estate, you need to know about the 1031 exchange.

Quick Story: Two clients of ours purchased a condo in the ski-town of Vail, Colorado, fifteen years ago. Their investment more than tripled and they wanted to sell, but not have to pay capital gains tax on the profit. They got in touch with our team and we referred them to a specific person that helps accommodate the 1031 exchange (so the clients are sure to stay on track with the specific terms and timelines needing to be addressed in order to be in compliance with the 1031

14   http://www.ronwebster.com/content/1031-exchanges-dummies

exchange process). They initiated the 1031 exchange, sold their home in Vail, and quickly purchased three other investment properties that were closer to their home in southern California. They essentially were able to diversify with three places as opposed to a ski-town condo. By buying at the time they did, we would expect that they would probably have the opportunity to do another 1031 exchange in a matter of years, and roll that amount of money into a commercial strip mall or multi-unit apartment building.

This is not a hard thing to do—it's rather easy, yet many investors don't know about it or don't care to learn. It's important to know not to get hung up on the word "exchange." The 1031 exchange—when I first heard about this, sounded to me as if you go find a home or another investment property to exchange or trade your properties with. This is not the case. The exchange is your way of showing the IRS you swapped out of one investment and "exchanged' it with another one. As a result, you don't have to pay taxes on this sale—it's a wonderful thing. There are certain rules you must adhere to, but there are interesting offshoots of the 1031 exchange, like a reverse 1031 exchange, where the purchase occurs first and you sell your place last. You can even do a 1031 exchange if you are taking a loss on the property so that you will not have to pay taxes on 1031 exchanges that occurred prior to the investment that is taking a loss.[15]

Whatever your exit strategy may be for your investment, you may wish to include the 1031 exchange as a vital tool and resource to reach your top investment potential and performance.

Substitute for paying for your kid's college room and board – Living in San Diego, I've seen and met several clients who had a child that

---

[15] http://www.irs.gov/uac/Like-Kind-Exchanges-Under-IRC-Code-Section-1031

was accepted into the local state university. Rather than having the parents fork over thousands of dollars for rent year after year, instead, they purchased a home directly in the vicinity of the college and have their kid act as the property manager for the two or three other roommates up until graduation. College rentals are always at a premium, and the roommates effectively subsidized the overall cost that the parents would otherwise have to pay to some other landlord to house their child (assuming they were paying for their child all along). Instead, not only did their kid's cost for room and board go down substantially, they also realized all the tax advantages that came with owning the investment property as opposed to just forking over their hard-earned cash to a landlord. Furthermore, the parents were able to sell the place for more than what they bought it for, once their child graduated. This should more than paid for their kid's education, leaving me to wonder why more parents don't do this. I assume that most cannot because the ability to pay their kid's tuition may be a feat in itself. However, if you are reading this book and have some children young enough to allow you to prepare for this in the future, you may wish to seriously consider it as a strategy to hedge against increasingly expensive college tuition costs.

Part II

Putting everything into Practice

Purchasing Your Investment Property, Due Diligence, Addressing
the Issues That Come up While in Escrow, and the Management
and Ownership of Your Property.

Let's assume since you have made it this far into the book that you
have the basic concepts down, are starting your search, and will eventually begin making offers on properties. With some luck and determination, through your search process, you will find a place (or places) that
will work for you as great candidates for your new investment property.
You write an offer and it is accepted—which is great—but you're only
half way there. The last half includes all your due diligence, inspections
and subsequent inspections, and requests for repairs along with properly
addressing all the other issues that may come up during the transaction,
prior to the close of escrow. Some of the issues discussed may not fully apply to every investment property, (you don't really need to do a property
inspection on a piece of vacant land you are investing in), but they should
apply to most of the investments out there. Here are some of the most
fundamental concepts to keep in mind, so you can utilize this knowledge
to your advantage and come out on top.

CHAPTER 8

Financials:

F OR ALMOST EVERY INVESTMENT—IT WILL BE 85% FINANCIALS AND 15% everything else, in terms of importance. It's all about the financials of the property which should make or break your investment decision. If you don't know what to look for or what makes a good investment in terms of the numbers, then this chapter is for you.

Numbers don't lie, and we need them to make certain justifications, assumptions, and inevitably a decision on whether a given property will work or not. After all, an investment property is a money-making machine—this machine can be a polished, well-oiled apparatus that works great, looks great, and just feels like a winner. This type of property commands the higher rents and looks to have little, if any, differed maintenance.

However, the opposite is also true and if the numbers aren't there, then neither is the value. Let's say, for example, that a landlord of a property for sale has very long-standing tenants that haven't had rent increases for some time. Since investment real estate is valued by the income the property generates, you will want to know how to compare it so that you can confirm the rents being collected are definitely lower than market. Also, you should know how to value the property assuming it was operating with market-rents in place. Essentially, you are projecting the rents for future performance. We use metrics all the time, not just to compare but to project certain returns on investments and to ultimately get very good at making assumptions as close to reality as possible. This section will get you clued in on the most important ones that we use all the time with investment property.

Some investment properties are very straightforward. If you are buying a single family home to rent out, you can pretty much do the basic computations to see the return on investment and cash flow analysis. The variables are few, and there's just one tenant to keep in mind. As your unit mix increases, the stakes increase proportionally, not to mention the price point, expenses, and potential issues with the people you are dealing with. This chapter is written with a multi-unit investment in mind. If you are purchasing a smaller place, much of this chapter will be overkill, yet, still very important stuff to know and apply for your future investments. With that said, lets dig deeper in some of the terminology, strategy, and tools for the financial analysis for any investment property you will be considering.

Cap Rates, Gross Rent Multipliers, Expense Ratios

What's a cap rate anyway? What's a Gross Rent Multiplier? What's the reason for an expense ratio? These are all metrics which people use to value and compare investment properties between one another.

A CAP rate stands for, Capitalization rate. It's like an expected return on investment of the underlying investment property. At the most basic level, it's the net return you get on a property after all expenses are taken into account. Take the annual net profit you make on a property (the annual positive cash flow after all expenses), and divide that yearly profit against the purchase price to get the CAP rate.

Quick Note: More specifically, the annual profit a property makes is known as your *Net Operating Income (NOI)*. You get this by taking all yearly income received from all the rents that you've taken in (this is known as your *Gross Scheduled Income)* and subtracting all expenses to get your total profit, or **NOI**.

Generally speaking, these numbers are all annualized, so if the rent is $2,000 per month and the expenses are $1,000 per month, then the GSI (Gross Scheduled Income) is $24,000 and the NOI (Net Operating Income) is $12,000. If the purchase price of the investment property were $120,000, then the CAP rate in this example would be .1, or 10%. (Divide $12,000 into $120,000.) Industry people would call this a 10 CAP.

A CAP rate is great because it tells you a bit about the property just by looking at one measurement.

My first real estate instructor always said that "the higher the CAP rate, the more risker the investment." Why would this be the case? It works similar to a bond in the financial market, where the highest returning bonds that you can purchase are the junk bonds. Similarly, the investment properties that you find with the highest CAP rates are usually the ones in the lesser (or least) desirable market areas that will be, harder to fill vacancies, or the property itself is in poor condition, or maybe a combination of both these issues. A property with the highest comparable CAP rate will be worth less and thus be offered for a lesser value. The property's rents that are collected will be most likely lesser as well, but the property's asking price will be so much lower that when computing the CAP rate, the lower price inherently makes the CAP rate rise substantially.

Contrast this to a premium investment property that has a lower CAP rate—essentially a lower rate of return. The reason it has a lower CAP rate is partially attributed to the fact that the underlying investment is most certainly going to be in a better area, meaning it's generally much more expensive. The tenants are typically of better quality and they will be paying higher rents, but the higher rents will be of a proportionally smaller increase than the overall asking price of the property. For this reason, the CAP rate is lower, but the underlying investment is more solid. In other words, less risky and more likely to be rented out and occupied. For this reason, you pay the premium for the more secure and valuable real estate. The increased premium means, a lower overall return of investment.

CAP rates can range from the low single digits to the high teens. Typically, you will find the best producing properties at a 3-6% CAP rate and the less desirable or riskier investments in the 9%+ CAP rate (if not higher). Therefore, if there's an investment property with a high CAP rate in a great neighborhood, then it's safe to throw a warning flag moving forward on that property.

Let's take an example with regards to a CAP rate. Consider the same property in two locations, one on the good side of town and the other on the lesser desirable side of town. Each property is a 4-unit building, all with 1-bedroom units, and the expenses are nearly the same. Because real estate is essentially valued based on the income a given property generates, the differentiation between these two properties are the rents that one makes over the other and overall value from one above the other. This is due in part to the different locations that affect the rental rates themselves. The rents for a one bedroom unit in the lesser desirable side of town top out at $900 a month, and the rents for the one bedroom in the more desirable of town are going for $1,200 a month. It doesn't seem like that big of difference, but it ends up being so. That $300 a month increase in rent, multiplied by the 4 units in the building, and multiplied again by twelve (for a year) means the property in the more desirable area, although it's the same size, generates $14,400 more in rent annually. (This is assuming we have no vacancy in a given year). While $14,400 may sound fantastic, you will end up paying much more for the more desirable location because of less perceived risk, and more perceived stability and the quality tenants themselves. A realistic purchase price, given comps and comparable CAP rates, for the lesser desirable location is about $550,000 and about $800,000 for the more desirable location.

In order to get the CAP rate, you need to know your total income and expenses and then divide by the purchase price. For example, let's say the annual expenses on the lower-end property are $20,000 and for the more desirable location, $25,000 (simply due to the fact that the higher priced property has higher property taxes and a minor premium on the maintenance). The CAP rate is determined by the following equation:

Gross Scheduled Income – Expenses / Purchase Price = CAP rate

Less desirable location:

$43,200 (Gross Scheduled Income: $900 monthly rent * 4 units * 12 months) - $20,000 (expenses) / $550,000 (given price) = **5.9% CAP rate**

More desirable location:

$57,600 (Gross Scheduled Income: $1,200 monthly rent * 4 units * 12 months) - $25,000 (expenses) / $800,000 (given price) = **4.0% CAP rate**

The more desirable location and real estate investment costs more and returns less. However, generally speaking, it's a more solid investment for the long-term because of its location, security in value, and ability and ease of renting out. Hence, its risk is limited comparatively, and therefore the return it provides reflects this. Although the higher priced property realizes higher rents, it won't be proportional to the premium you pay in overall purchase price. The trade-off is that you invest in a location that has a good deal of opportunity to continue to appreciate and be more desirable, as well as having fewer problems with finding quality tenants to fill a vacant space—in other words, less risk and thus more solid investment for the better located property. It's all about location first and foremost.

In the same way a blue-chip stock may have a low, yet consistent and dependable dividend compared to the potentially high return, yet risky junk bond or penny stock, in real estate, location is the key. Therefore, the better the location ensures the safer investment; however, you have to pay more to get this, because the overall risk is limited, you can expect proportionally lower returns.

Better quality location usually has an effect on the tenants you rent out to as well—it's an intangible aspect of your investment analysis. However, the better the location means the better the tenants. Generally, that implies a better chance to have tenants respect the property without you having to evict anyone. Eviction may be a rarer occasion in nicer areas, but it may be the status quo in less desirable neighborhoods. The point is, you get what you pay for, and there's nothing different when it comes to investment real estate.

CAP rates are good to know because it helps you to compare one property to another. An investment in one part of town can be the same property but have quite a different CAP rate as another property you are considering at the other end of town. The difference is the income each property generates, which, in addition to expenses, creates the variables that make up a CAP rate. From this, you can compare the pros and cons of each property to make the best, informed decision possible.

Sometimes you can see that a place is beaten up, and that a decent investment in cleaning and fixing up a place would allow a new owner to increase rents. Opportunities such as these should at least be considered, as they have the potential of being profit-generating investments. You can compare other similar properties that have been fixed up to see what they take in for rent. Then make an assumption on the rents that you can get for your place once fixed up. Use the going CAP rate for that comparable property (or gross rent multiplier—see below) to get a sense of after repair value.

Gross Rent Multiplier – This term is a metric similar to the CAP rate in that investors use it to judge and compare values of one property to another. It's used less frequently than the CAP rate, but it's still an easy measurement and good to know.

How to get a Gross Rent Multiplier? Divide the price of a property by the annual rent revenue (Gross Scheduled Income) it generates. For example, a $500,000 investment property that generates $50,000 GSI a year has a Gross Rent Multiplier (GRM) of 10. GRM is used a lot more for investment properties of 4 units or less. As you get into bigger investment properties, the pros like to use CAP rates for the most part, as the GRM doesn't take into account expenses. This is a vital component on the performance of a piece of investment property and therefore gives the CAP rate more weight. However, when it comes to 2-4 units, I like using the GRM to quickly assess the general value of a place and if it makes sense given the price being asked. We use GRM a lot in the 4 unit or less properties because at this size, the expenses are fairly consistent and redundant.

Example: San Diego tends to have a lot of multi-family property, mostly in the neighborhoods surrounding downtown and less so in the beach and coastal communities. We can test, value, and compare prices for a 2-on-1 property in one of the neighborhoods that surround downtown, and we find that Gross Rent Multipliers are ranging between 10 and 16 in these areas. If we were to take one such property and see that its GRM is 15, we can use this as a basis of comparison. Then if this inland property is a GRM of 15, it's good to see what duplexes are selling for in and around the beach, for a comparative example. The Gross Rent Multiplier for the coastal property should be higher given the desirability of the location near the coast. Because of the coastal proximity location, the rents and property prices are proportionally higher, therefore, so should be the Gross Rent Multiplier (GRM). When checking the beach and coastal areas, we find the average GRM for a duplex is about 18-20, which supports the value of the other unit near downtown that has a GRM at 15. If it were the other way around, this would be a warning flag that the inland property is potentially over-priced because the GRMs for similar properties in more-desirable beach communities should be higher.

Expense Ratio

Although there is no hard and fast number, typically we like to see an expense ratio of no more than 50% and ideally in the range of 25-40%. Expense ratio is the amount of expenses relative to the income generated. In that case, a place that rents for $10,000 a month shouldn't have more than $5,000 in expenses each month. Ideally, the lower the better, because the lower the expenses, the more profit the investment is generating each month for you.

Bringing it all together:

If the property is being managed very poorly, it should have a high expense ratio of above 50-60% of GSI, and there should be expenses that can be cut out completely as a result. Doing so would do two things: Firstly, the expense ratio goes down due to increased efficiency of the underlying asset. Secondly, the lesser amount of expenses means the property will take in more profit. That means the Net Operating Income (NOI) would increase, which also increases your CAP rate as well. A higher CAP rate means an increased return on investment, as well as the fact that the property is now more valuable due to the additional income. This example assumes that you already own the place. Otherwise, you wouldn't be able to make these changes in the way the property is run before the close of escrow. By being able to increase efficiency from an expense standpoint, you not only alter the return on investment but you also increase the CAP rate. This justifies a higher asking price if you were inclined to sell shortly after your purchase.

Increasing rents would have a similar effect. That is why some investors buy a property they know can withstand rental increases, perhaps because the current tenants are paying below market rents by a nicer-than-necessary landlord that hasn't increased rents over a long period of time, through means of improving the property and upgrading to justify a higher rental amount, or a combination of both. The higher rents effectively increase the Net Operating Income and that investor can then sell for substantially more.

Quick Example: If a 4-unit property was purchased at a 6% CAP rate, and you were able to either, reduce expenses of the property or increase rents (or both) that resulted in the tune of $200 a month more income per unit, how much more does that value the property, given the 6% CAP? What you do is take the new total annual additional income, and divide by the CAP rate—that $200 * 4 units * 12 months = $9,600. Take that $9,600 newly realized income, and divide by .06 (6% CAP rate) to determine and project the increased value in the property due to the $200 per month, per unit improvement in the income (or re-duced expense, or both), and you get $160,000 in increased property value. A little change can make a BIG difference.

You can use the CAP rate equation interchangeably to your benefit. Find out if a property in question is priced right versus others. Find what a property will or can be worth given improvements, or see what a prop-erty is worth just based on plugging in a hypothetical CAP rate. Use this freely and the more you play with the numbers, the easier and more fun it gets.

Other key metrics

Sometimes you may hear of Internal Rate of Return and Cash on Cash investment return. Usually, these metrics have to do with the money that has actually been invested (the investors "skin in the game" versus the profit realized). These terms are more advanced concepts, so I'll leave them for another time and place—but please be reassured that depending on your comfortability with mathematics, it may come to you naturally. If it doesn't, don't fret, we make it simple and easy in this book. If you do wish to know more regarding Internal Rates of Return, as well as de-preciation and recapture analysis, among other more intensive-financial variables, consider working with a financial advisor, your CPA, another professional investor, or the Realtor assisting you in the search that has internalized these concepts. They can mentor you accordingly in an effec-tive and real time manner.

BONUS: We have included at the end of the book, a re-source where you can be given a Pro Forma spreadsheet for help in computing all of these terrific new metrics and con-cepts, as well as a glossary of terms.

CHAPTER 9

Expenses, Who Pays and how much

XPENSES ARE KEY—HAVE TOO MANY AND YOUR RETURNS ARE REDUCED
to little—or nothing at all, even negative! It's incredibly important
to understand what you are getting into, identify any warning flags
that come from the financial analysis, and determine if you are buying a
decent investment or not.

Expenses are all of the regular and irregular costs to run and operate the property. For a single home or condo, it's pretty straightforward,
but once you get into multi-unit, apartment, and commercial buildings,
you involve the costs of the debt service (mortgage payment), utilities,
taxes and insurance, gardener and maintenance, advertising, trash fees,
pest control, management fees and legal/professional fees, and upgrades,
among other minor items that arise from time to time.

Tracking and monitoring expenses is the key. What makes it difficult
is that these differ from property to property. Here are some key things
you can do to compare and analyze expenses of a potential investment
property you are considering:

1. Ask the seller/owner (or their agent) if these expenses have been
    around the same throughout their ownership, on average. Question
    any particularities.

2. If possible, call the local utility company and see the history of the
    expenses for that given property—ensure they have been consistent
    throughout recent history to avoid any surprises.

3. Call and check on other similar properties for sale in order to com-
    pare notes and to ensure the expenses that are stated for the subject

property are reasonable and more or less in line with what else you are seeing and reviewing.

4. Take note of your personal experience of what maintenance and utility expenses are and extrapolate proportionally to the investment property you are considering.

5. Consider ways to reduce expenses. You could, manage the property yourself, consider energy upgrades, or perhaps, install new low-flow regulators on all sinks and showerheads in your property to reduce your water expenses. Find creative ways to net more money. Consider installing a coin-operated laundry machine for added income. Consider shopping around for the insurance policy or adding and bundling of the insurance policies that you already have for increased savings. Maybe a different gardener can be used for less money. The more creative you are will mean more money in your pocket at the end of each month.

6. Ask the seller about any major capital improvements that have been made to the property lately that make the expenses look higher than necessary. Specifically, ask the owner what they would do next to the property, if they had the money to do so. This may help to prepare and plan for what will need to be done to the property, as opposed to it becoming an unforeseen surprise repair expense.

When it comes to what's typical for who pays the utilities, it's completely up to you and how you arrange the leases with the tenants you rent to. You can also discuss this with the current property manager or discuss alternative strategies with a potential new property manager. With that said, tenants usually pay for their gas, electric, and telephone. If there's any one utility the landlord usually pays for, it's the water bill. This is usually because any given multi-unit property doesn't have multiple water meters and the bill cannot be split up fairly and equally. It is possible to modify an existing system with individual sub-meters to each unit, but the maintenance and monitoring of this and billing may be overly expensive and not realistic. Other than the water, I'd always advise to have your tenants pay for everything themselves because otherwise, they are not incentivized to conserve their usage and overall carbon footprint.

Putting all the expenses together with the intended and expected income allows you to project the return on investment—this is what we call a **Pro Forma.**

CHAPTER 10

Making a Pro Forma? What to take into account:

He Pro Forma, when put together appropriately, will project how a property and investment will perform given certain assumptions. A Pro Forma can be a couple calculations or a complex spreadsheet. It takes all variables into account and projects cash flow, CAP rate, depreciation, tax rate, Internal Rate of Return, etc. The sky's the limit.

At the most basic level, you plug in what you are paying (purchase price), how much you are putting down as down payment, record the expenses, record the rent/income received, realize the net profit (or loss), and project this out into the future. You can also take into account cost increases (because energy, water, and the gardener all get more expensive over time), as well as a vacancy factor to take into account (a loss of income due to a rare occurrence of not having your place(s) rented out). All of this gives you a more accurate and refined sense of how your money machine should be performing well into the future.

What we like to do is put a separate Pro Forma together for all properties being considered in order to compare them accordingly, looking at their CAP rates, and readily adjusting the variables as necessary. In total, we can see where the investment stands when compared to other properties being considered. This will help to allow the best financially performing asset to surface to the top of your list of which property to consider making an offer on.

BONUS: As a bonus for purchasing this book—we offer a standard Pro Forma free for your use—check out the book's website for this essential and useful tool for your property search.

Whenever I work with investor clients, I always put the variables into a Pro Forma and send it to them to consider the return of investment and analysis of the numbers for the property in question. When the input numbers are unavailable (such as certain costs for utilities, management, advertising, maintenance, etc.), I then make an assumption, and let the client know that at the end of the day, this is a professional projection, but based on what other similar properties expenses have shown.

With a solid template to make a Pro Forma (we use excel spreadsheets as they are quick and easy) you can quickly and easily analyze the investment properties that you are considering, using the financials as the main basis of analysis.

Analysis and Adjusting

Now that you've put together a Pro Forma for your investment property— always know that this is a work in process; here are some things to keep in mind when considering the financials and analysis of a given property:

Keeping in mind rents, historic vacancy, etc.

Making sure the rents are true and accurate is part of your due diligence when researching and looking into the property during your inspection period. You should be getting the "rent-rolls" early into the inspection period, while in escrow, from the seller , and be able to ensure the property actually realizes and takes in the rents they are saying it does. The complexity of this report comes down to the management. If the property is being professionally managed, then perhaps you can expect a QuickBooks-like professional looking report and accountancy of the "rent–rolls". Sometimes if the place is being self-managed, at worse, you'll be getting bank printouts and other somewhat crude methods to verify the property is generating the income that has been stated. Even if they are bad managers, they still report this property's workings on their tax returns, so they have to have *something* on hand. Any particularities will and can come up with review of this information—inquire about any inconsistencies, any continual late payments, and current past due accounts, or anything that seems other than business as usual. These will serve to highlight any potential opportunities from current inefficiencies by the current owner's management, as well as knowing any problem tenants to focus on replacing as soon as it's legally appropriate to do so.

The due diligence period is also a good time to review the leases and rents individually to see how it compares to other units in the general vicinity. Determine if there is upward mobility and potential to increase rents.

Sometimes tenants who have been in place for some time have not had their rent rise as much as other units that change tenants every year. I've seen tenants who have been in their unit and renting a place out for nearly twenty years, and the landlord just didn't feel right to increase that tenant's rent to what other people were paying in the same complex. When you see this, although you may not want to kick that tenant out, you will know there is upward mobility in the rental amount for that particular unit. Most of the time these tenants will expect what is coming and they are usually amenable to a rental increase that would seem appropriate— after all, it's either this place or somewhere else at the same or similar rent, and moving is not something that anyone likes to do.

Checking on historic vacancy is important. How easily does the place rent out? What has the seller/owner done in terms of marketing and advertising, if any, when they rent the place out? Do they put out a sign? A Craigslist posting? What they do and the ease, lack of time, and money in doing so will indicate exactly how easy it is to get their place rented out, and if there needs to be a cost associated with this on your Pro Forma. This reminds me of a few examples regarding the sequence, process, and ease of getting your place rented out:

I was representing a buyer on a property that was really close to downtown San Diego. It resembled a boarding home on steroids where there were ten rooms that were rented out on a weekly basis with a minimum stay of one month. Just two shared bathrooms existed for all ten rooms and their inhabitants. The place was very well managed, and in order to get the place rented, they placed a sign in the lawn, made a post on Craigslist, and found a renter that afternoon—no need for an advertising budget when it's that easy. This was surprising because I was not expecting that kind of response due to the way this place was laid out (you wouldn't think a weekly rental would be so popular, but it was), and since the rents were reasonable for the landlord and the tenant alike, this is the response the new owner now comes to expect.

Another example has to do with a duplex I helped a client purchase on a main road next to one of our major universities in town. My clients purchased the property within days of the new semester starting. We thought this was perfect timing but it ended up being too late. By that time, for the most part, all students had found their place for the semester, and it took a couple months to get both places rented out. This was a surprise because we were expecting these places to be rented out within days, but it took several weeks.

In both cases, it's important to analyze all sides of the investment, even the impression or intended response you would or could have from the target tenant pool. Identifying the strengths and weaknesses of each place will help immensely when planning and making assumptions, especially when it comes to finances and rent ability of your investment property, as well as the need for advertising budget expense on your Pro Forma. It's better to be safe than sorry. If you identify a potential issue in the rent ability ease for a given property—or if you recognize the property will need three to four weeks of work before it is ready to rent, you can take all expenses and hard costs (the mortgage/holding costs, the repair/ improvement costs, and the lack of rent upfront) into account. This will help to create a more accurate financial picture (Pro Forma) for the property at hand.

Deferred maintenance, cost of maintenance, and age of building as part of the equation in your analysis.

It's important to keep in mind that no property is ever perfect. Even brand new homes have defaults that need to be addressed, so most certainly anything you look at will need some degree of work. Given that the average age of all homes in the U.S. is approximately 1974 construction[16], properties will almost always have deferred maintenance; these include costs that will need to be taken into account at the very beginning of the purchase, and other items that may come up in the short-term after escrow closes. The age of the building must be at the top of your mind when you are doing inspections. If the property you are purchasing is over forty years old and the sellers haven't replaced their main drain line, there is a good chance the clay or cast-iron sewer pipes have reached their life expectancy. You should budget this potentially high-ticket repair item accordingly.[17]

Unfortunately, unless the item or issue at hand is failing at the time of the inspection and causing a health or safety issue, more often than not, the seller expects you to accept the property and its condition as-is. That is the case, even if the roof has just a year or two left, or the pipes are on their last leg, or the electric is dated (but working). It doesn't preclude the sellers to make any repairs or give credits for these issues unless there are current, significant faults and/or health or safety issues with respect to the home. Even then, it's up to the sellers to agree to make concessions. Take notes, do additional inspections where you see fit to see exactly where you

---

[16] http://infocentral.blogs.realtor.org/2013/05/14/rural-versus-urban-average-age-of-homes-and-much-more/
[17] http://psinspection.com/blog/?p=692

stand, modify the Pro Forma accordingly, and analyze the property from there. See if it's still as reasonable and attractive as it was when you first laid eyes on the property.

For Condos & Complexes, Be Mindful of potential issues with the HOA, cost increases, CC&R's etc.

If your investment property includes an HOA or is in a condo complex, or if it's a shared community with an agreed set of rules to live by, please understand that you cannot control what you are getting yourself into. Sometimes you'll move into a home and it turns out that your neighbors are awesome, and sometimes it's the exact opposite. The same is true for HOA's. It's very easy to have a belligerent HOA owner's board, crotchety personas that are difficult to deal with on everything and are very used to the word "NO", and there isn't anything that can be done about it without getting directly involved by becoming a board member yourself, which may not be the highest and best use of your time.

On the flip side, the HOA can be amazing, and we hope it will be for you. There is a good chance that if your investment is a single family home or condo, it will be affiliated with some sort of an HOA. In fact, over half of the owner-occupied homes in the U.S. today are governed in some form by an HOA. [18] It's a necessary evil, but HOA's are an easy way to manage a lot of people in a small space. Nevertheless, it's best to address any potential issues or problems with the HOA before you own the property. We've found the most effective way to find out about the inner workings of the HOA is through engaging with some of the nearby neighbors living within the HOA in question. We always do this when showing property. Without fail, anytime a neighbor is asked about their complex, they will open up like a book without hesitation. This strategy alone has saved several thousand dollars for our clients and we highly recommend it!

---

[18] http://psinspection.com/blog/?p=692

CHAPTER 11

The property inspection

A landlord is showing a couple around an apartment. The husband looks up and says, "Wait a minute. This apartment doesn't have a ceiling." The landlord answers, "That's OK. The people upstairs don't walk around that much."

- Gilbert Gottfried

WHAT HAPPENS WHEN YOU FIND A GREAT PROPERTY, MAKE AN offer, and go into escrow? Now it's time to do the property inspection, which is done the same time you are reviewing your disclosures and reviewing financials—this is considered your due diligence period. However, many times with investment property, it's typical where no showings are allowed until there has been an accepted offer. For many investment properties, the first time you actually see inside is when you already have made an offer that has been accepted and you're in escrow.

Why is this common? As it's often the case, first time investors find it strange or weird that with many residential rental income properties, you can't actually view the place until you've written an offer, negotiated the main terms, and find an acceptance with the seller. In all actuality, this is the common method of doing business and it actually makes sense to do so in this way. It's because the tenants in the property have to be involved with the sale, and we want to ensure that the transfer of ownership causes the least amount of turbulence for them. For example, how would you feel as a tenant to constantly have to keep your place open, available, and tidy for strangers interested in becoming your new landlord for days and weeks and possibly months on end? You could see that if a tenant was inconvenienced several times just to show the properties to all interested parties, it would be excessive enough for them to vacate the property altogether. Sometimes simple logistics make this impossible. Imagine trying to line up a showing for an interested buyer for a 10-unit apartment complex. Can you imagine the agent trying to set up the showing, hoping that a single time works for a dozen different parties, and then doing this each time a new interested buyer comes along? For this reason, it's why we only show the properties to serious buyers who are qualified potential new owners for the property. That's the way it goes in most instances and it seems to work quite well. Going about it this way creates palpable motivated sentiment with the buyer and this is reflected in having so much interest that you make an offer on the place first and then see what's going on inside (literally and figuratively), after all parties have reached acceptance. After all is said and done, as the new owner you may want to retain most or all of the current tenants—it would be a shame for the transfer process and sale to go so poorly that the tenants all give their notice and leave. Then you would have to start from scratch upon the close of escrow. In my experience, tenants want to be kept in the know and be dealt with fairly and with respect and honesty. They want to have the least disturbances and least changes as possible from beginning to end of the sale of a property. With this in mind, it will give you insight into how to treat these tenants accordingly when you take full ownership of the property.

Upon acceptance, you line up the inspection through the assistance of your agent. Sometimes, we have clients that don't see the value of doing a home inspection and would rather save the couple hundred dollars by doing an inspection themselves to satisfy their concerns about the subject property. To that I would say, don't be such a cheapskate! The reason some buyers think this way is that they incorrectly associate zero value to having a professional home inspection performed. I've heard the stories where someone has had an inspection done, and from what they see, it looked so easy, they thought they could do a good enough job or better themselves. To these clients, the inspector checked a couple of plugs, poked around a bit, but overall didn't provide anything of value. I would say perhaps that this inspector might have been a dud, but not all inspectors are created equal. I believe the process and value of knowledge found through the inspection will not just bring you some peace of mind about the place you are about to buy, it will also highlight the most pressing items that may need to be addressed early on in the ownership. Things will have a negative effect on cash flow for your new property and we highly recommend doing an inspection no matter what. Even better, you can use this information about these deferred maintenance issues (if any) to your advantage by submitting a repair (or credit) request for the conditional safety-related items found through the property inspection to the seller.

In rare instances, the inspection may reveal something that is such an insurmountable issue that it would ruin the deal altogether, forcing you to cancel the offer and walk away. Although this is rare, it does happen. Without paying the couple hundred dollars for the property inspection, the client would not have been able to dodge the bullet. Instead, they have inherited a problem property.

Inspectors that we typically work with usually have a few thousand dollars of equipment, testing devices, and many, many years of experience. They do this every day and see patterns of potential issues with homes of a certain era. Everything they do is beneficial to you as the buyer, so it's something that we recommend. Even clients of ours who are general contractors would get a professional home inspection just so they have a second pair of trained eyes to take a good hard look at the property. You will want to do this as early as possible in the escrow process. Your agent can help assist in referring good people, if you don't already have a great inspector, as well as facilitating any secondary inspections that are recommended from the initial general inspection.

Warning flags! During inspection

The property inspection will help uncover the most pressing issues and items of concern for the property you are looking to buy. Also, keep in mind any other potential warning flags the property has, as well as verifying the numbers/financials that have been advertised with respect to the property.

- How does the general look and feel of the property seem to you? This will help uncover potential deferred maintenance.

- Do you see any shoddy repairs or repairs done by the tenants themselves? This may be a sign that the seller has been unresponsive as a landlord and there will be other issues and items that may come up.

- Check the parking for each unit. Does it add up as advertised? Will there be any issues?

- Check the alleyways in back (if any) and the neighboring properties. Are there bars on all the windows and/or graffiti? This will be a sign of potential issues with renting out as well as the types of tenants you will find—as the tenants will be looking at and comparing the same things.

- Be sure to verify the rents as advertised compared to what was actually collected. You will (or should) be getting copies of all the books, leases, and other supporting documentation that talk about the property. Study them because now is the time where you have an opportunity to ask all the questions.

- Check the local police reports to see if the property or area surrounding is a problem or riddled with crime.

- Ask neighbors about the property and the location in general, if they are available. Their information is invaluable for your confidence or concern with the property in question. Neighbors generally *love* to talk—you may find out more information than you originally anticipated. Always take information with a grain of salt; you don't get the full truth all the time from tenants, so practice asking weighted questions that will get you the answers you seek without the life story from the tenant(s).

- There will be a lot of information, but don't freak out if you find a piece of information or evidence that is not great. It doesn't mean you need to pull the plug, unless the issue at hand is severe in nature to substantially reduce the value of the property, or the seller is unwilling to reasonably concede on value as a result.

Most importantly, establish rapport with the tenants immediately. Engage them in a professional manner during the inspection and remember to ask them about the owner and how good a job he/she/they have done as a landlord (it's typical that the owner/seller won't be at the inspection so the tenants really do open up). Ask about their experience as a tenant, finding out what's wrong with, not just their unit but also, the property in general. You should find out how they like living there, what they would do differently, and what they would want to see addressed if you could waive a magic wand and have it done. This way, you can find out specific things to look for during the remainder of the inspection, as well as knowing what you will want to improve or have done to the property at the onset of your ownership, not just to increase morale with your new tenants but for the betterment of the property as well. This exercise should not be a buddy-buddy type of dialog with the tenants, but you do want to come off likeable. You want to hear out their concerns and pay them respect, while at the same time extracting all the best information.

Whenever you are engaging the tenants, always remember to do so with a grain of salt; they will mostly be forthcoming but sometimes they can exaggerate the situation and circumstances to get special attention or favors from their new, would-be landlord. Surely, the sellers and listing agent will paint the best picture when it comes to the property, but in my experience it's been the tenant's brutal honesty that provides valuable insight into a given investment property. It has proven quite helpful for all our investor clients. Nevertheless, don't ever believe anyone 100%. Trust, but verify all later.

Most of the time this information is found when everything is happening on inspection day, and sometimes it can be accomplished by asking permission to engage the tenants specifically, if you were unable to do so on inspection day. By being intentional in your interaction with the tenants, it can give you a great idea of the overall health of the property, how well it's been managed and maintained, provide insight to current and potential problems, as well as determining whether the current tenant(s) is one you wish to keep around or not. However, sometimes you won't be able to engage with the tenants very much or at all. As a result, you need to move forward in the best manner possible. Ask questions to the seller in regards to the tenant history and anything that sprang up from your review of the inspection, financials, and disclosures.

Request for Repairs (or Credits)

If the inspection finds an issue with the roof, then you will want to get a roofer out there for a subsequent inspection. If an issue is found with the plumbing or electrical, then it is best to get the plumber or electrician to go out and check the issue. They can submit to you a report on that particular issue, as well as an associated estimate or bid to correct the issue(s) at hand. Once you have the estimate, you have an idea on what you can go back to the seller with. The intention of doing so will be to renegotiate a lower price or get a credit from the seller for closing costs. The theme to any request should be with fairness in mind. If the roof has a year or so left on it but is still functioning, that doesn't mean that the seller "owes" the buyer a new roof; however, it's very appropriate to get a good deal of the total cost of the roof credited to you (if possible), given the condition of the roof itself. Using your agent to help guide you and getting a feel for how the seller(s) negotiate will help give you the sense on where to push and where to pull back in this renegotiation process. We have found that the type of market that you are in also has an effect on these negotiations as well, where if it is a buyer's market, sellers will be more accommodating than if it's a seller's market. Nevertheless, we have found that everything else being equal, most sellers want to be fair, and as long as you are fair with them in your dealings and requests, you can expect them to be reasonable and cooperative in return.

You can typically ask the seller to do repairs as opposed to getting a credit, but in most cases, we wouldn't recommend sellers doing repairs. Let's say the roof is shot and you request the seller fix the roof. The incentive for the seller is to use the cheapest outlet possible and not the best person for the job (because the best is usually more expensive). For very minor repairs, you may find that it's easier to just have the seller oversee the repairs. In almost all cases, we recommend the buyer ask for credits in lieu of any repairs being done and oversee the repairs themselves once they own the property.

A note on owner repairs: Watch out! Many times the owner *themselves* will opt to do requested repairs. We would strongly vote against this from happening. In our repair requests, we usually request that a licensed, bonded, and insured professional or contractor handle any repairs. This usually takes care of the seller not doing the repairs themselves. In one transaction, we had a seller that was an active contractor who was licensed, bonded, and insured. He insisted that he be the one to repair an exterior staircase as opposed to having this done by the termite company that would otherwise do the work. If the seller did it his way, he would save around $8,000. Because the buyers wanted to get this concession accepted, along with a few other items, they did agree to have the seller do those repairs. The buyers took a big risk in doing so, because if the seller did the work incorrectly, it could potentially ruin the deal. We had to tread lightly and be very specific in the overall scope of work and insisted that everything be done appropriately without any corners being cut. It was a stressful process to confirm with the city that the proper permits were pulled and the work was done according to codes. At the end of it all, we made it work out. However, if we had to do it all over again, I would have preferred to have the seller not involved with any of the repairs.

Sometimes the seller is an institutional investor and they are flipping the property or they have a contractor that regularly services the property and is intimately knowledgeable about the property—if this is the case, then it may be acceptable to ask the seller for repair requests. This is a rare exception because in this instance, the sellers will find it more advantageous to do the repairs themselves and have a team already in place to do the work and do it well. The sellers are contractors/flippers and do this professionally, so they will be very well suited to get the work accomplished to an acceptable degree. They would most likely not be doing the work themselves but their sub-contractors or workers will be doing it. In most cases, we have found this was a decent route. The buyers got what they wanted and it was a relatively inexpensive cost to the sellers, as opposed to them granting a much larger credit for the same amount of work that they could do for less.

Sometimes a repair is out of the question given the price you were able to get the property for, or the market itself makes it so that the buyer's requests for repairs are not agreed to. If a seller gets fifteen offers and accepts yours, and then you come back to the seller with a $10,000 credit request for roof repair, the seller may cancel your request and ask you to take the deal and the property as is. Otherwise, he can go back to the pool of buyers that made offers, to see who will take the property as-is.

The point is, no transaction is ever the same, and there is no blanket statement in real estate, save ethical and legal standards by the people and professionals involved. However, this gives insight on what to do and what to expect when it comes to your inspection.

CHAPTER 12

Prorations of Rents & Deposits in Escrow

JUST LIKE WHEN YOU BOUGHT YOUR FIRST PLACE, WHERE THE PROPERTY taxes were prorated by the escrow company overseeing the transaction, so too will the property's rents and security deposits. For example, if you purchase a place and it closed in the middle of the month, then half of all the rents and all of the security deposits on file would be credited to you at the close of escrow. This is good to know because it can be used as a negotiation tool in some cases.

Quick Story: About a year ago, we were working with a luxury high-end client looking for beach property. The place we found that he liked the most had a tenant in the home until the end of the year. That tenant prepaid their rent for the entire year, and the monthly rent was $5,000, so nearly $30,000 was going to be transferred or credited to my client the day he would close escrow on the property (for the remaining months of rent on file and paid for by the current tenant). This was great news for the buyer as he wouldn't want to move until the beginning of next year anyway, and whereas he was seemingly unwilling to go u p in price at the onset. He changed his tune once we secured the fact that he would be covered on the rent until the end of the year and would be compensated for $30,000 because of it. He wasn't willing to go higher until he found this out. Knowing things like this and asking the right questions may change things for the better for you, too. We ended up negotiating a lower price in addition to getting that rent prorated and transferred to him at the close of escrow.

This is important to know, and keep in mind that there is a chunk of money that will be transferred to the new buyer at the close, especially in cases where there are several units and several security deposits held in trust. Use this to the best of your ability when negotiating, but do remember that those security deposits need to be on hand when your tenants eventually move out!

CHAPTER 13

Things to Prepare for and Consider Prior to Renting Out Your Investment Property:

S O YOU'VE CLOSED ESCROW ON YOUR INVESTMENT PROPERTY AND now it's time to get your place rented out. For most first time investors, people like to take things into their own hands and do the property management themselves. I am a fan of professional property management, but sometimes it's good to experience this process at each step of the way to learn the basics. Regardless, we want to ensure that your place is ready to rent, and you will want to get the place spic and span as soon as possible, once you have closed escrow. In some cases, you may purchase an investment property without any immediate need to fill vacancies, which is great. However, you can use this initial period of ownership to construct a plan of action when tenants do move out, or a plan on what upgrades and improvements to install in the property in general, and when. There is a good chance the property could use a new paint job and get the flooring cleaned (or even replaced). Most places aren't perfect, and this will be known from the inspection process that you have just gone through. Renters know this too; they aren't expecting the Taj Mahal. However, the money you invest to beautify your place will translate into a property that will rent more quickly and maybe for above market, depending on what you do.

Improvements

Going back to what we said at the beginning of the book, it's import-ant to not get overly emotional or too attached to your new place. The same thing goes when it comes to getting your place rent ready. If you need to update and improve your investment, remember this is not a place you will be living in. It's a rental, and the wear and tear from tenants will eat away at any additional income you may be getting from above average improvements.

Quick Example: Instead of the nice hard wood, go for a laminate. It's ¼ of the price, and many times as durable. You will go through many a tenant before you need to consider replacing the laminate flooring. Instead of above average appliances, get new lower-end appliances (and this is according to your rental). Obviously, if you have a rental in an above scale neighborhood, you want to hover around what's expected for that area. Therefore, if the area is a neighborhood of lavish and upgraded homes, you should have reasonable appliances that fit the type of target renter you are going for. However, never overindulge, ESPECIALLY because you won't be able to enjoy it. Granite can be very inexpensive these days, so go for the builder standard instead of a Formica countertop— the tenants will love it. It will last longer and you'll get higher rent for the upgrade.

Quick Tip: Beige and off-white is your friend—Neutral and earth tones are fantastic for rental property. Not too dark, and not white enough to show off every scuff and scratch in the floors and walls. When it comes to repainting and redoing the interior cosmetics, go beige for your home!

BONUS: As an added bonus for the purchase of this book, go to the website and get a punch list of the easiest to-do's to get your place rent-ready in the least amount of time for the most amount of rent.

Property management is your friend

If you have tried to be a property manager before and are "over it," then you need a professional property manager. Property management is your friend, and if you don't know why, you would soon find out when managing a property yourself. After a few late-night or weekend service calls, endless QuickBooks entries, and constant visiting of the property to fix random items, many see the value in the "cut" that property managers get from your rents.

It's great to interview and meet a few property managers. There are several and they are not all equal. Here are some important questions to ask when interviewing potential property managers for your investment property:

- How long have they been in the industry? (we suggest at a minimum 2 years of experience)

- Current portfolio—how many units and volume are they overseeing? (you don't want too many, or too little)

- Are they managing properties similar to the one you have, to make it easier for them to rent out?

- Are they licensed, bonded, certified, and have the industry accolades and designations?

- Do they specialize in your particular niche of property?

- Are they close by (for ease of response time)?

- How do they market their available rentals? Ask to see some current examples to see if they're tech savvy and to see if their internet marketing is satisfactory. Because nearly all rental searches begin online, having a good handle on the online marketing and tech presence is necessary for any property manager today. If it's difficult to find their current listings and advertising online, what does that say about when they try to advertise your place online?

- How do they go about screening the rental applicants to be sure they are properly analyzing potential tenants? Are they doing a credit check? Background/criminal check? Verifying Funds?

- Do you like them? Has the communication with them and follow up on their part been sufficient?

Not all property managers do the same service, so ask for a blank or sample agreement assuming the answers to the above questions are sufficient to merit your consideration of their services. See what they do, the expectations that they set, and how much they are asking for in compensation.

How much is too much?

Typically, you can expect a property manager's fee to be between 6% and 10% of the gross amount of rents received each month for single-tenant properties. As the property gets larger and the units increase in number, their fee gets smaller and smaller—for example, the fee to manage a 40-unit apartment complex may be 3-5% of the gross rents received each month.

I highly encourage the use of property managers just for the peace of mind and efficiency on their part. They are well worth the money. They have the connections to repair people to take care of issues when they go wrong or if something needs to be fixed. They tabulate and account for all expenses for you, which makes it easier for tax purposes, and they allow you to focus on what you do best. By all means, if you are willing and you have the time, go for it! However, anything more than one unit to rent out, then I personally believe that property management is the way to go.

If you are just renting one unit, or if you wish to have a go at managing property yourself, here are the best tools and resources that we have found for owners looking to rent their place out quickly:

Craigslist

Although many have complained about Craigslist and the litany of scams that reside within the confines of this website, it's still, in my opinion, the best and easiest go-to website to get the word out about your rental. They have since upgraded their user interface to show results on a map to compete with other sites. The reason why it's so good is because MANY people still utilize it as a go-to resource for rental property. If you are using a property manager to professionally manage your property, make sure they use Craigslist and see some current places they are listing there to get a good idea of how savvy they are with their online marketing.

Rentometer, Hotpads, Zillow, Padmapper, Postlets and other like apps and websites

There will always be new and improved sites and cutting edge technology that outpaces and leapfrogs over the current resources available. But in today's market, we have a couple go-to favorite sites as resources for our investor clients, when it comes to analyzing the rent being asked by a potential investment property.

Rentometer.com – Type in your address, what you are renting out, and for how much. This website will analyze your rent and compare to the other rentals nearby to see if you are low, high, or just right.

Hotpads.com – This is a good rental website for advertising that gets a lot of traffic. (this website is now owned by Zillow – see below)

Zillow.com – Mostly known for real estate values and homes that are selling or buying. The site also features rentals and you can promote an open house here for a rental when looking for a new tenant.

Padmapper.com – This site is a great tool that bundles the rentals being listed on many other sites, and places them on one easy to navigate interface. This is good to compare rent prices and see if your place is being rented for a competitive amount.

Postlets.com – Also part of the Zillow Group and like Padmapper, Postlets can syndicate to other sites. You can do a ton of other stuff as well, like push to Facebook and twitter, and send the Postlets interface in a ready for Craigslist HTML code to copy and paste right into Craigslist. Then your Craigslist ad isn't a painfully archaic amalgamation of typescript and blank space, but a fresh looking layout with pictures and colors. All good stuff!

Using these services all at once is not overkill. Rather, it gives you the most bandwidth to reach a larger group of potential people. These are also the best resources to compare your place to other properties to see if your rents are low, at market, or too high.

CHAPTER 14

Strategies and Best Practices on Renting Your Place Out:

Pricing

D EPENDING ON THE AMOUNT AND TYPE OF MARKETING YOU ARE doing, you can analyze the market response to determine if you are asking too much (or too little) rent. I usually base this on the amount of calls and inquiries you get, especially in the first week after you start advertising. There is no silver bullet for going about doing this, but if your phone is ringing off the hook, or you are getting emails and text messages up the wazoo, then you can determine that you are asking too little in rent. If your place has been on the market for a week and you haven't gotten a single inquiry, then you know you are overpriced. I aim to get a couple inquiries a day. This tells me that we are in the right zone for what we are asking. However, many renters are fickle—they talk a big game. When push comes to shove and you need them to fully draft out an application, state bank accounts, personal history, have a guarantor of the lease and get a credit check (if necessary), it becomes a natural deterrent to many would-be bum tenants. In other words, the initial reaction may be great, but the key is how many serious inquiries you can get that actually go through the process of submitting a full application. This can be a lot of work upfront, which is even more reason to hire a property manager.

What forums to advertise in?

I'll it say again, I love Craigslist. The paper is a dying marketing tool and too expensive. You can advertise freely on the internet, so that's what I like to do— always utilize the resources that are fast, cheap, and easy.

We mentioned a few great sites above that specialize in rentals. There may even be a great (free) local community website or bulletin board(s) online to advertise on as well.

Depending on the demand and the speed of your local market, an open house may be a good idea to save you valuable time and have your place available to be seen by a lot of people in a specific period of time. I recently did this with one of our rental properties. The local rental market was very hot and within a 2-hour open house on a Sunday, we had fifty people come through, twenty-four people took applications, and I got seven applications back—three of which were phenomenal tenants. It gets hard to choose the best one, but at the end of the day, this is a quality problem to have and this method of marketing was the most efficient for my time schedule. Marketing the open houses on Craigslist and the previously mentioned websites from the last chapter are necessary.

Ask the previous landlord what worked the best—sometimes it's as easy as sticking a sign in the lawn. Many of our clients have purchased properties in such prime locations, or on such prominent streets that all it took to fill a vacancy was a simple "for rent" sign in the lawn. Also, a newspaper advertisement may actually pay off—depending on the circumstances. For a rental investment in the high-priced beach community of Coronado (the island adjacent to downtown San Diego), the Eagle Journal is their local publication and it is THE best way to get a rental filled—surprising to me, but true. Obviously, these strategies must be tailored to your local area, but my goal here is for you to see a couple of solid strategies and do a bit of research on your own to find out what will work best for your situation, target demographic of your tenant, and location. Remember, it cannot hurt to ask the previous owner what worked best for them. Sometimes this can be solid gold knowledge that they took years to find out and they will tell you for free.

Rental Applications and Tenant Screening:

You will want to properly qualify your potential renters. The better job you do of this upfront, the less problems you will have during the length of the lease—I cannot stress this enough—be diligent with the screening and analysis of your tenants. You will want to use a standardized rental screening form, which you can get from a local real estate board, Office Depot, or from the internet. The more thorough the document is the better. In addition to rental applications, encourage the tenants to provide proof of funds and any other information they believe will be helpful in the proper determination of their candidacy as tenant for your property. Keep in mind that each state has different landlord and tenant rights, rules, and obligations. This advice is by no means legal advice, nor should this ever be construed as condoning discrimination—everyone should be given an equal shot; the only thing you can be discriminating with is their financial well-being and their credit report. That's why it's so important to include a credit and/or background check while doing the due diligence on a potential renter.

BONUS: Look in the Bonus section at the end of the book for a California Dept. of Real Estate example of a rental application.

One of the best and easiest sites we use is https://www.mysmartmove.com/ —this makes it easy for landlords to quickly verify the credit status and criminal history of a potential renter. Many times renters pay an "application fee" to a landlord for a credit report along with their application, never knowing if the landlord actually got the credit report or not. It can get messy. My Smart Move (by Transunion) has the tenants sign in and pay the service online themselves and they get to see the results as well as you, the landlord. You see their credit and criminal history profile and the system gives you a green thumbs up or red no-way for the tenant in question. It's easy, reasonable, and very efficient. If you are self-managing, we highly recommend this program, but if you are using a professional manager, make sure they use something similar. They should have the best technology available.

No matter what, a little work upfront can go a long way. Make sure you are putting the best people in your property so that:

- Rents are paid on time.

- The tenants take good care of the property.

- Little deferred maintenance.

- No need to evict or serve notice.

- Fewer "issues" or complaints, in general.

- Good tenants and good landlord-tenant relationships result in long-term tenants.

- Less likelihood of you missing a rent payment.

Sometimes, you may even want to price your offered rent a smidge under market rent, to get the best of the best, as opposed to charging the highest possible rent and having a revolving door of renters each year. Think long-term and think things through. If you have a partner in this investment, talk it over and develop a golden rental philosophy—be tough yet fair and professional. Include some of the techniques in this and the next chapter and you will be sure to have happy and qualified tenants in your rental property, which should, in turn, make you a happy and smiling landlord.

CHAPTER 15

Ownership, Maintenance, and Protecting Your Investment:

How to hold property

f this is your first property, it may make sense to hold the property in your name. Depending on the property, and your overall net worth (or planned future net worth), you may want to consider an alternate strategy of ownership for your asset. This would insulate you from liability as well as protecting your asset in the event of a major asset-loss event.

In other words, you need to protect yourself from the property itself, in case anyone trips and falls on the property and wants to sue you for it. You also need to protect the asset from being absorbed or garnished as a result of an unrelated incident where you are losing your worth considerably (for example, divorce, lawsuit, etc.).

In the event you are sued based on the result of something that happened on the property, most people think their insurance will cover the damages. However, what happens when you reach the maximum that your insurance covers? Let's say that someone trips on a crack in the driveway on your investment property and injures themselves considerably. You have insurance that covers up to $1 million in liability, but the person sues you and wins $1.5 million in court. You are now responsible for that $500,000 in the event that you own the property in your name only. Perhaps you can purchase an "umbrella" insurance policy that will supplement additional insurance in the event something happens or someone gets hurt on any of your properties. Another way to address this issue is to hold the property's ownership in a (or as a) separate legal entity, such as an LLC.

If the property is being owned and held in an LLC, then the person suing you can only sue and win assets for as much as all the assets that are held in the LLC itself.

Quick Note on the LLC: For this to work, the LLC must be owned by you, and you maintain all of the records, keep meeting minutes, and follow all the directives that an owner of an LLC must do. That includes paying the yearly LLC fee so that you are in compliance. Not paying would be the easiest and biggest mistake. Most lawyers would probably check this first; in the event of any issue regarding someone attempting to protect themselves with this type of legal-entity veil.

In other words, whatever is in the LLC is up for the taking if the individual who is suing you wins in court. They may be awarded $1.5 million. If the insurance covers $1 million, and the property itself is only worth $200,000—that's pretty much all the person is going to get, since the LLC is then bankrupt. You insulate yourself from liability in this example. This is also a great example as to why most people who own more than one property, and have considerable assets, should consider an umbrella insurance policy to cover in events where the insurance doesn't cover everything that could possibly go wrong.

If the property is being held as an LLC and you are sued as an individual, it may still be accessible because of your lawsuit. That's why you may want to consider creating a living trust, who would essentially own the LLC. That way, if you were sued as an individual, the suing party could not access the assets contained in the LLC that owns your property, because it's being held in a trust that's completely separate from you, as an individual, and depending on the type of trust that you have created. Having layers of legal entities can no doubt become expensive, not to mention the attorney's fees in creating these structures, but when you need them you are VERY happy that you have them in place.

Please note that I am not a lawyer. These are merely examples - possibilities of strategies that you can incorporate into the ownership of your properties and assets. Of course, you will want to connect with the appropriate professional, an asset preservation attorney, a trust attorney, etc., to properly assess your situation and if/how you can benefit from some of the ideas stated herein. By no means is this meant to be construed as legal advice and all states have differing laws, practices, and standards. Please consult the necessary professional when it comes to matters such as these.

No matter what, in order to get the most out of your investment, you need to make sure that you are properly protecting the property and yourself at the same time, throughout your course of ownership.

You will want to make a habit of meeting with or calling your attorneys, financial planners, and CPA's, etc., at least once a year (generally towards the end of the year), to make sure you are taking full advantage of all tax strategies relative to your ownership. Confirm that you are fully protected to the most reasonable extent possible from liability, as well as making sure they are all privy to any changes that have taken place in the past year (added inhabitants, refinanced property, changed ownership into a trust, changes to the tax code that effect you, etc.). When it comes to this kind of stuff, you can never be too safe. And you do want to invest a decent amount into accredited, dependable, and trustworthy professionals that you can develop a long-term relationship with—this is the true pathway to total success!

Open a bank account specifically for your investment, for ease of financial planning and taxes purposes too.

One of the smartest things to do as soon as you purchase your new investment is to open a new bank account specifically for the new property you own. All income, expenses, and transactions should be conducted through this singular checking account in order to keep everything completely separate. Not only does this make things easier from an expense perspective, but it also contains all financial aspects of the property in one bank account, which makes things easier for clarity, transparency, paying and tracking expenses and for tax purposes. You should also get a debit card for the account to make things even easier when it comes to paying on expenses for the property. If you have a property manager, they can direct deposit the income into your account each month. Essentially, this is a free thing to do and saves a lot of time and confusion when it comes to properly documenting and analyzing your investment property. If you get more property, make an account for each investment property you own.

CHAPTER 16

Property Management & Treating
Your Tenants Right = A Happy Property

Strategies for Best Practices with Your Tenants:

WHEN IT COMES TO WORKING WITH YOUR TENANTS, IT'S IMPORTANT to be tough, yet fair. Far too often the most common complaint I hear from landlords is that they are "too nice" to their tenants. When you are too nice, your tenants will more than likely take advantage of you. You never think they will, and you believe that if you are nice or a team player, that your tenants will respond with respect in return. This is not normally the case. Tenants and renters tend to take as much free reign as possible. They will do as much as they can get away with and try not to be caught. They can be expected not to do, act, or behave the way you should or would be expected to. Not all tenants are like this, but it's the ones who are that stick in the mind of landlords and serve as a turning point example. Those landlords say, "never again."

It's important to be clear and assertive with tenants, just like an employee and employer relationship. Also, it's important to set expectations and emphasize the importance of the contractual agreement that is the lease they entered into. Make sure you understand the lease agreement so that you can speak intelligently and with knowledge when it comes to issues that may arise throughout the renting of your property. More than anything, it's important to be tough, yet fair when dealing with your tenants. That way they will know that they won't be able to get away with anything. I don't want to come off as overbearing or pessimistic concerning your tenants' relationship; by all means, you want this to be a harmonious business relationship. If you choose right and act professionally, you shouldn't have any issues. I just don't want you to become one of those landlords that say, "I shouldn't have been so nice."

While you continue to manage your property with a disposition of tough fairness, you can do certain things to convey that you care in a way that won't be taken as a weakness to your tenants:

- Remember your tenants' birthdays, send a birthday card, and maybe even a small gift. This small effort and gesture goes such a long way. If your tenants feel that you care, then it will build trust and maybe they will want to take better care of the property. If not their birthday, then consider a pie delivered a day before Thanksgiving.

- Remember your tenants' kids and pets' names—another simple gesture for them to see you care.

- If you aren't having professional management, take care of the property, it's VERY important to address every inquiry that comes from the tenants with respect to the property. Issues that are not properly addressed convey a lack of care on the part of the landlord. It also means there is a chance that there will be a lot of deferred maintenance.

- Deferred maintenance is not your friend—if it's broken, then fix it right the first time and avoid the duct tape fix. The duct-tape fix will not make the tenants happy and they will keep calling each time the issue resurfaces. You don't want to be a "slum-lord," but that doesn't mean you have to spend an arm and a leg on every issue that comes up. Be an informed consumer and do the repair the right way.

- A text message has a 99% chance of being seen and read by the receiver of that text. You may want to send a courtesy notice a day before rent is due and again the day before a late fee is to be levied. Chances are you will get rent on time, more often with less excuses.

- At the end of the day, your tenants just want to be respected and felt cared for. If this is the case, then they should respond and care for your property in the same manner, assuming you rented it out correctly. If you didn't rent it out correctly, and your tenants are not taking care of your property and respecting you, then it's time to serve your tenants notice and find some new ones.

Note: You never want to have to serve notice or evict a tenant, but this may happen to you from time to time. Before it does, you may want to align yourself with an eviction specialist in your area, who can help serve proper notice and file the necessary paperwork to the court in the legally correct manner. This does cost money, sometimes upwards of $1000+ to get the served notice and documentation filed, but it's well worth it to learn about the process if you haven't gone through this yourself before. Ask questions, see what documents are filed, understand the timelines, and you may be able to handle the process on your own if it happens again and save the money. However, the best practice for you as a first time investment property owner is to hire a professional eviction service to assist you when you need to evict a tenant and learn from there as opposed to learning on the fly and trying to go at it yourself the first time; this would be the wisest possible choice.

CONCLUSION

Bringing it All Home

NSIGHT AND ANALYSIS FOR THE FUTURE OF INVESTMENT REAL ESTATE has never been more bullish—over the past many years, we have not been building very many homes and have a supply shortage throughout the entire country. We didn't stop having babies during this time, and properties that were too old to continue standing needed to come down, given a natural rate of replacement. We have a situation where we have a lot more people needing housing that aren't necessarily ready, able, or willing to purchase a home, yet they need to find a place to call home. There is a prolonged built-up demand for rental property throughout the country because of the resulting situation of the economic downturn experienced from 2007 to 2012. It's not going to end anytime soon, and with people still struggling to make ends meet (most aren't buying homes because they can't qualify for a loan), it means that a landlord can expect multi-family properties and investment rental real estate to do quite well in the short, medium, and long-term.

We aren't making any more earth, so we have to work with what we have. This means more density, more urbanism, and a greater need for affordable housing. By being an investment real estate owner, you can essentially profit nicely by taking advantage of this sociological and economic trend that we are in, and I expect we will continue to experience this for many years down the line. Real estate and investment real estate are looking great as avenues for investors, small and large, to invest in, and you ought to take full advantage as opposed to being left in the dust with regret from missed opportunities.

Investment real estate is a great way to supplement and ensure a happy, healthy, and wealthy retirement. One investment property will not necessarily make you rich, but if you pay it off or do it again and again to create a solid portfolio or nest egg, you can create a small fortune in a relatively short amount of time and do so while maintaining your day job and current standard of living. There is no easy way to wealth, and investment real estate is no different. By no means should this wealth-building strategy be viewed as a get-rich-quick scheme, but it has been demonstrated by many different people throughout history as a viable way to build wealth and help to live comfortably for years and down lineages of family heritage. Anybody can do this if they take the time and follow the principals and guidelines outlined in this book.

By now, you have been informed on exactly how to start your journey of investment property ownership. You know how to test each property you are considering by using the IDEAL system of checks and balances to ensure the property you are considering makes sense. You know the main concepts to keep at the forefront of your mind when considering your ideal property. Whether it's a home, condo, multi-unit property, or some other investment property type, you now know the different options and types of investment properties out there to consider, as well as how to go about mastering the niche-style and investor-type you can work towards becoming. You're now more accustomed on when to buy, where to buy, and how to go about researching the right way to make the most informed decision possible.

You've been educated and informed on how to go about doing the purchasing of a property. You know what financial metrics are and why they are important. You know what to look for, how to compute returns, and compare the analysis from one property to another to determine what the better buy is. You know now how best to go about the actual purchasing of the property and what to look for while in a transaction.

You know the best practices on managing and overseeing your investment. You know what to do, and who to hire to see your investment thrive and produce at its highest potential. You know the best ownership and legal/liability strategies to help protect you and your assets at the same time. You've learned about the hurdles, pitfalls, and how to go about addressing them in the best possible manner to help you win with your investment goals.

All in all, what took several years to comprehend has been reduced to what you've just read. Quite honestly, this is not rocket-science. My best advice is, since you have read this book, go get started . . . now! There is no time like the present and what I've found is that those who take action are the ones who are generally rewarded. Like the game of life, the laggards and procrastinators lose out in investment real estate. As long as you utilize the tools and resources demonstrated in this book, you will no doubt find success in your ventures. It may not be the first time around—you may have to make offers on a lot of places to get one, but it all starts with one, and you build it from there. Nobody was ever born a professional. We all must start somewhere, and where you end up is entirely up to you. I hope you take the content and concepts throughout this book to heart and begin your process of building your real estate investment portfolio. It's my sincerest hope that this book helps you get into the landlord class of society. It's a wonderful thing when you can have other people pay your mortgage while you profit and build wealth in the process. It's a fantastic strategy to employ along with stocks, mutual funds, IRA's 401(k), and the like. The timing couldn't be better and it's a great thing to do, yet many don't because of the perceived barriers to entry. Hopefully, this book has knocked down some of the real barriers, as well as perhaps the psychological barriers, that may have hampered you in earnestly getting to it with regards to finding your first investment property. Here's to your success for today, tomorrow, and for the future.

RESOURCE SECTION
Standard Pro Forma for analyzing property:

Go to:

www.thefirsttimehomeinvestorbook.com

For a resource and link to a standardized real estate investment Pro Forma that you can use to reference as well as referrals to other investment sites that offer up a decent Pro Forma analysis tool.

A Pro Forma will allow you to analyze investment property; project cash flows, project rents, and help you to make the best most logical decision for your investment at hand.

Finding a great Realtor or lender referral:

Go to:

www.thefirsttimehomeinvestorbook.com

For a resource to link you with a great Realtor or lender (or both) throughout the US & Canada that can do a great job in assisting you with your first time investment purchase. We refer through our solid network of professionals that are the respective pros in the industry for the area they serve and we can refer for most every city in the country.

Let us know where you live and we will source for you a professional real estate and/or lending professional within forty-eight hours. We only refer the best and will vet the referral prior to your introduction.

RENTAL ENHANCEMENT CHECKLIST

Rent-Ready Punch list

A quick list of the easiest to-do's to get your place rent-ready in the least amount of time for the most amount of rent.

You've decided to rent your home!

When renting property out, it's important to look at your home from a different perspective, the renter's perspective.

The Home Enhancement Checklist provides you with insight and direction on how to get the most rent for your home by making minor changes and repairs.

GENERAL

Tidy up!

☐ When a home appears cluttered tenants can't "see" the home or its potential. By storing items you don't need or use, your home will feel more inviting to potential renters. When renting a home, less is more!

Clean up!

☐ A clean home gives the impression that it has been well cared for.

☐ Strive to make your home visually and aromatically appealing.

☐ Remember: Paint is worth $20 in the can, but it's worth $1000 on the wall!

Patch up!

☐ Minor repairs often become major stumbling blocks for potential tenants. Take away those distractions by fixing minor issues before they become major.

The finishing touch!

☐ The little "extras" make a home feel special.

☐ Remember, your home is competing with others in your neighborhood. Make your home stand out!

THE EXTERIOR Tidy up!

☐ Mow the lawn, trim trees and shrubs away from the house, rake leaves, pull weeds, and dispose of dead plants, and flowers

☐ Clear up any rubbish around the home

Clean up!

☐ Wash windows, inside and out

☐ Sweep all sidewalks and driveways

Patch up!

☐ Repair doors and windows

☐ Repair major cracks in sidewalks and/or driveways

☐ Repair roof shingles, shutters, gutters, windows, siding and fencing.

☐ Leaks are the most common problem for rental property

☐ Clean up the front/back yards with new sod, plants, flowers and mulch if needed

The finishing touch!

☐ Add a doormat at the entrance

☐ Add a potted or hanging plant

☐ Add new house numbers

THE KITCHEN Tidy up!

☐ Clear extra gadgets from all kitchen countertops

☐ Remove all messages, pictures and magnets from the refrigerator

☐ Clear away any papers, mail or newspaper that may have accumulated on countertops

☐ Clear sink, stove and countertops of all dishes, pots and pans

Clean up!

☐ Wipe down cabinets & polish sinks

☐ Clean all appliances, inside and out

☐ Wash kitchen floors

☐ Air out garbage area with a deodorizer and/or freshener

Patch up!

☐ Repair any faucet/sink leaks

☐ Repair any broken appliances

☐ Repair any non-working kitchen cabinets and drawers

☐ Patch and paint, walls, and ceilings, if necessary

The finishing touch!

☐ Add a new throw rug and a plant

THE BATHROOMS

Tidy up!

☐ Remove any unnecessary items from the countertops

☐ Organize linen closets, medicine cabinets, etc.

Clean up!

☐ Clean sinks, toilets, bathtubs and showers, and make sure they are mold-free. Polish mirrors and bathroom fixtures and wash bathroom floor.

Patch up!

☐ Repair any faucet, sink and/or toilet leaks. Caulk and grout tile, if necessary. Patch and paint walls and ceilings, if necessary

The finishing touch!

☐ Add a scented candle

☐ Add a new shower curtain

Additional observations:

_____

_____

_____

THE LIVING AREAS

Tidy up!

☐ Remove piles of papers and magazines from tables

☐ Straighten bookshelves

Clean up!

☐ Clean and deodorize all carpet, spot cleaning where necessary; wash all floors

☐ Wipe down lighting fixtures, making sure all light bulbs are working

☐ Wash window treatments and clean fireplace, if applicable

Patch up!

☐ Patch and paint walls and ceilings if necessary

The finishing touch!

☐ Install a scented freshening agent for the living space.

☐ (if staging) Rearrange pictures to highlight specific areas. Add lamps if room is dark

THE BEDROOMS

Tidy up!

☐ Remove extra furniture and rearrange to define areas

Clean up!

☐ Clean and deodorize all carpet, spot cleaning where necessary

☐ Wash window treatments

☐ Wipe down lighting fixtures, making sure all light bulbs are working

Patch up!

☐ Patch and paint walls and ceilings, if necessary

The finishing touch!

☐ Add decorative pillows to beds

☐ Add a plant

THE BASEMENT AND GARAGE

Tidy up!

☐ Organize all areas: laundry area, family area, workshop, garden equipment, etc.

☐ Box up and store or dispose of any unnecessary items

☐ **Clean up!**

☐ Sweep and clean floors

☐ Remove cobwebs from walls, window sills and ceilings

☐ Wash windows, inside and out

Patch up!

☐ Make sure furnace, A/C and hot water heater are in working order

Additional observations:

_____

_____

_____

HERE COMES A RENTER...

☐ Before each showing, be sure to complete these last minute touches to make your home standout and look great!

EXTERIOR

☐ Pick up after pets

☐ Pick up lawn tools, toys, etc. lying around the yard

☐ Clear driveways and walk areas

INTERIOR

☐ Open curtains for daytime showings and close curtains for nighttime showings

☐ Open windows to "freshen up" your home

☐ Do a quick tidy up

Additional observations:

_____

_____

_____

AM/

PM. Tenant shall vacate the Premises upon termination of the Agreement, unless: **(i)** Landlord and Tenant have extended this Agreement in writing or signed a new agreement; **(ii)** mandated by local rent con**4. RES**

RENTAL APP

An Example of a (California) rental application & lease.

CALIFORNIA ASSOCIATION OF REALTORS®

RESIDENTIAL LEASE OR
MONTH-TO-MONTH RENTAL AGREEMENT
(C.A.R. Form LR, Revised 12/13)

Date_____, _____ ("Landlord") and
_____ ("Tenant") agree as follows:

1. PROPERTY:

A. Landlord rents to Tenant and Tenant rents from Landlord, the real property and improvements described as: _____ _street, _ _____ ("Premises").

B. The Premises are for the sole use as a personal residence by the following named person(s) **only:** _____ _____

C. The following personal property, maintained pursuant to paragraph 11, is included: _____ _____ or ☐ (if checked) the personal property on the attached addendum.

D. The Premises may be subject to a local rent control ordinance _____ .

2. TERM: The term begins on (date) _____ ("Commencement Date"). (Check **A** or **B**):

☐ A. **Month-to-Month:** and continues as a month-to-month tenancy. Tenant may terminate the tenancy by giving written notice at least 30 days prior to the intended termination date. Landlord may terminate the tenancy by giving written notice as provided by law. Such notices may be given on any date.

☐ B. **Lease:** and shall terminate on (date) _____ at _____ ☐ AM/ ☐ PM. Tenant shall vacate the Premises upon termination of the Agreement, unless: (i) Landlord and Tenant have extended this Agreement in writing or signed a new agreement; (ii) mandated by local rent control law; or (iii) Landlord accepts Rent from Tenant (other than past due Rent), in which case a month-to-month tenancy shall be created which either party may terminate as specified in paragraph 2A. Rent shall be at a rate agreed to by Landlord and Tenant, or as allowed by law. All other terms and conditions of this Agreement shall remain in full force and effect.

3. RENT: "Rent" shall mean all monetary obligations of Tenant to Landlord under the terms of the Agreement, except security deposit.

A. Tenant agrees to pay $ _____ per month for the term of the Agreement.

B. Rent is payable in advance on the **1st (or** ☐ _____ **) day** of each calendar month, and is delinquent on the next day.

C. If Commencement Date falls on any day other than the day Rent is payable under paragraph 3B, and Tenant has paid one full month's Rent in advance of Commencement Date, Rent for the second calendar month shall be prorated and Tenant shall pay 1/30th of the monthly rent per day for each day remaining in prorated second month.

D. PAYMENT: Rent shall be paid by ☐ personal check, ☐ money order, ☐ cashier's check, or ☐ other _____ , to (name) _____ (phone) _____ at (address) _____ , (or at any other location subsequently specified by Landlord in writing to Tenant) (and ☐ if checked, rent may be paid personally, between the hours of _____ and _____ on the following days _____). If any payment is returned for non-sufficient funds ("NSF") or because tenant stops payment, then, after that: (i) Landlord may, in writing, require Tenant to pay Rent in cash for three months and (ii) all future Rent shall be paid by ☐ money order, or ☐ cashier's check.

4. SECURITY DEPOSIT:

A. Tenant agrees to pay $ _____ as a security deposit. Security deposit will be ☐ transferred to and held by the Owner of the Premises, or ☐ held in Owner's Broker's trust account.

B. All or any portion of the security deposit may be used, as reasonably necessary, to: (i) cure Tenant's default in payment of Rent (which includes Late Charges, NSF fees or other sums due); (ii) repair damage, excluding ordinary wear and tear, caused by Tenant or by a guest or licensee of Tenant; (iii) clean Premises, if necessary, upon termination of the tenancy; and (iv) replace or return personal property or appurtenances. **SECURITY DEPOSIT SHALL NOT BE USED BY TENANT IN LIEU OF** PAYMENT OF LAST MONTH'S RENT. If all or any portion of the security deposit is used during the tenancy, Tenant agrees to reinstate the total security deposit within five days after written notice is delivered to Tenant. Within 21 days after Tenant vacates the Premises, Landlord shall: (1) furnish Tenant an itemized statement indicating the amount of any security deposit received and the basis for its disposition and supporting documentation as required by California Civil Code § 1950.5(g); and (2) return any remaining portion of the security deposit to Tenant.

C. Security deposit will not be returned until all Tenants have vacated the Premises and all keys returned. Any security deposit returned by check shall be made out to all Tenants named on this Agreement, or as subsequently modified.

D. No interest will be paid on security deposit unless required by local law.

E. If the security deposit is held by Owner, Tenant agrees not to hold Broker responsible for its return. If the security deposit is held in Owner's Broker's trust account, and Broker's authority is terminated before expiration of this Agreement, **and** security deposit is released to someone other than Tenant, **then** Broker shall notify Tenant, in writing, where and to whom security deposit has been released. Once Tenant has been provided such notice, Tenant agrees not to hold Broker responsible for the security deposit.

5. MOVE-IN COSTS RECEIVED/DUE: Move-in funds made payable to _____ shall be paid by ☐ personal check, ☐ money order, or ☐ cashier's check.

Category	Total Due	Payment Received	Balance Due	Date Due
Rent from _____ to _____ (date)				
*Security Deposit				
Other				
Other				
Total				

*The maximum amount Landlord may receive as security deposit, however designated, cannot exceed two months' Rent for unfurnished premises, or three months' Rent for furnished premises.

Tenant's Initials (_____) (_____)   Landlord's Initials (_____) (_____)

© 2013, California Association of REALTORS®, Inc.

LR REVISED 12/13 (PAGE 1 OF 6)

| Reviewed by _____ Date _____ |

EQUAL HOUSING OPPORTUNITY

RESIDENTIAL LEASE OR MONTH-TO-MONTH RENTAL AGREEMENT (LR PAGE 1 OF 6)

Agent: Michael Wolf   **Phone:** 858-722-6847   **Fax:** 619-923-3201   Prepared using zipForm® software
Broker: Ascent Real Estate Inc,410 Kalmia   San Diego   ,CA 92101

Michael Wolf

123 Sample street

Premises: _____ Date: _____

6. LATE CHARGE; RETURNED CHECKS:

A. Tenant acknowledges either late payment of Rent or issuance of a returned check may cause Landlord to incur costs and expenses, the exact amounts of which are extremely difficult and impractical to determine. These costs may include, but are not limited to, processing, enforcement and accounting expenses, and late charges imposed on Landlord. If any installment of Rent due from Tenant is not received by Landlord within **5 (or ☐ _____) calendar days** after the date due, or if a check is returned, Tenant shall pay to Landlord, respectively, an additional sum of $ _____ or _____ % of the Rent due as a Late Charge and $25.00 as a NSF fee for the first returned check and $35.00 as a NSF fee for each additional returned check, either or both of which shall be deemed additional Rent.

B. Landlord and Tenant agree that these charges represent a fair and reasonable estimate of the costs Landlord may incur by reason of Tenant's late or NSF payment. Any Late Charge or NSF fee due shall be paid with the current installment of Rent. Landlord's acceptance of any Late Charge or NSF fee shall not constitute a waiver as to any default of Tenant. Landlord's right to collect a Late Charge or NSF fee shall not be deemed an extension of the date Rent is due under paragraph 3 or prevent Landlord from exercising any other rights and remedies under this Agreement and as provided by law.

7. PARKING: (Check A or B)

☐ **A.** Parking as follows: _____

The right to parking ☐ is ☐ is not included in the Rent charged pursuant to paragraph 3. If not included in the Rent, the parking rental fee shall be an additional $ _____ per month. Parking space(s) are to be used for parking properly licensed and operable motor vehicles, except for trailers, boats, campers, buses or trucks (other than pick-up trucks). Tenant shall park in assigned space(s) only. Parking space(s) are to be kept clean. Vehicles leaking oil, gas or other motor vehicle fluids shall not be parked on the Premises. Mechanical work or storage of inoperable vehicles is not permitted in parking space(s) or elsewhere on the Premises.

OR ☐ **B.** Parking is not permitted on the Premises.

8. STORAGE: (Check A or B)

☐ **A.** Storage is permitted as follows: _____

The right to separate storage space ☐ is, ☐ is not, included in the Rent charged pursuant to paragraph 3. If not included in the Rent, storage space fee shall be an additional $ _____ per month. Tenant shall store only personal property Tenant owns, and shall not store property claimed by another or in which another has any right, title or interest. Tenant shall not store any improperly packaged food or perishable goods, flammable materials, explosives, hazardous waste or other inherently dangerous material, or illegal substances.

OR ☐ **B.** Except for Tenant's personal property, contained entirely within the Premises, storage is not permitted on the Premises.

9. UTILITIES: Tenant agrees to pay for all utilities and services, and the following charges: _____ except _____ , which shall be paid for by Landlord. If any utilities are not separately metered, Tenant shall pay Tenant's proportional share, as reasonably determined and directed by Landlord. If utilities are separately metered, Tenant shall place utilities in Tenant's name as of the Commencement Date. Landlord is only responsible for installing and maintaining one usable telephone jack and one telephone line to the Premises. Tenant shall pay any cost for conversion from existing utilities service provider.

10. CONDITION OF PREMISES: Tenant has examined Premises and, if any, all furniture, furnishings, appliances, landscaping and fixtures, including smoke detector(s).

(Check all that apply:)

☐ **A.** Tenant acknowledges these items are clean and in operable condition, with the following exceptions: _____

☐ **B.** Tenant's acknowledgment of the condition of these items is contained in an attached statement of condition (C.A.R. Form MIMO).

☐ **C.** **(i)** Landlord will Deliver to Tenant a statement of condition (C.A.R. Form MIMO) ☐ within **3 days** after execution of this Agreement; ☐ prior to the Commencement Date; ☐ within 3 **days** after the Commencement Date.
(ii) Tenant shall complete and return the MIMO to Landlord within **3 (or ☐ _____) days** after Delivery. Tenant's failure to return the MIMO within that time shall conclusively be deemed Tenant's Acknowledgment of the condition as stated in the MIMO.

☐ **D.** Tenant will provide Landlord a list of items that are damaged or not in operable condition within **3 (or ☐ _____) days** after Commencement Date, not as a contingency of this Agreement but rather as an acknowledgment of the condition of the Premises.

☐ **E.** Other: _____

11. MAINTENANCE:

A. Tenant shall properly use, operate and safeguard Premises, including if applicable, any landscaping, furniture, furnishings and appliances, and all mechanical, electrical, gas and plumbing fixtures, and smoke alarms, and keep them and the Premises clean, sanitary and well ventilated. Tenant shall be responsible for checking and maintaining all carbon monoxide detectors and any additional phone lines beyond the one line and jack that Landlord shall provide and maintain. Tenant shall immediately notify Landlord, in writing, of any problem, malfunction or damage with any item on the property. Tenant shall be charged for all repairs or replacements caused by Tenant, pets, guests or licensees of Tenant, excluding ordinary wear and tear. Tenant shall be charged for all damage to Premises as a result of failure to report a problem in a timely manner. Tenant shall be charged for repair of drain blockages or stoppages, unless caused by defective plumbing parts or tree roots invading sewer lines.

B. ☐ Landlord ☐ Tenant shall water the garden, landscaping, trees and shrubs, except: _____

C. ☐ Landlord ☐ Tenant shall maintain the garden, landscaping, trees and shrubs, except: _____

D. ☐ Landlord ☐ Tenant shall maintain _____

E. Tenant's failure to maintain any item for which Tenant is responsible shall give Landlord the right to hire someone to perform such maintenance and charge Tenant to cover the cost of such maintenance.

F. The following items of personal property are included in the Premises without warranty and Landlord will not maintain, repair or replace them: _____

Tenant's Initials (_____)(_____)   Landlord's Initials (_____)(_____)

LR REVISED 12/13 (PAGE 2 OF 6)

Reviewed by _____ Date _____

RESIDENTIAL LEASE OR MONTH-TO-MONTH RENTAL AGREEMENT (LR PAGE 2 OF 6)

rental app and lease for

144

123 Sample street

Premises: _____ Date: _____

2. **NEIGHBORHOOD CONDITIONS:** Tenant is advised to satisfy him or herself as to neighborhood or area conditions, including schools, proximity and adequacy of law enforcement, crime statistics, proximity of registered felons or offenders, fire protection, other governmental services, availability, adequacy and cost of any wired, wireless internet connections or other telecommunications or other technology services and installations, proximity to commercial, industrial or agricultural activities, existing and proposed transportation, construction and development that may affect noise, view, or traffic, airport noise, noise or odor from any source, wild and domestic animals, other nuisances, hazards, or circumstances, cemeteries, facilities and condition of common areas, conditions and influences of significance to certain cultures and/or religions, and personal needs, requirements and preferences of Tenant.

3. **PETS:** Unless otherwise provided in California Civil Code § 54.2, no animal or pet shall be kept on or about the Premises without Landlord's prior written consent, except: _____ .

4. ☐ (If checked) **NO SMOKING:** No smoking of any substance is allowed on the Premises or common areas. If smoking does occur on the Premises or common areas, (i) Tenant is responsible for all damage caused by the smoking including, but not limited to stains, burns, odors and removal of debris; (ii) Tenant is in breach of this Agreement; (iii) Tenant, guests, and all others may be required to leave the Premises; and (iv) Tenant acknowledges that in order to remove odor caused by smoking, Landlord may need to replace carpet and drapes and paint the entire premises regardless of when these items were last cleaned, replaced, or repainted. Such actions and other necessary steps will impact the return of any security deposit. The Premises or common areas may be subject to a local non-smoking ordinance.

5. **RULES/REGULATIONS:**
   A. Tenant agrees to comply with all Landlord rules and regulations that are at any time posted on the Premises or delivered to Tenant. Tenant shall not, and shall ensure that guests and licensees of Tenant shall not, disturb, annoy, endanger or interfere with other tenants of the building or neighbors, or use the Premises for any unlawful purposes, including, but not limited to, using, manufacturing, selling, storing or transporting illicit drugs or other contraband, or violate any law or ordinance, or commit a waste or nuisance on or about the Premises.
   B. **(If applicable, check one)**
      ☐ 1. Landlord shall provide Tenant with a copy of the rules and regulations within _____ days or _____ .
      OR ☐ 2. Tenant has been provided with, and acknowledges receipt of, a copy of the rules and regulations.

6. ☐ (If checked) **CONDOMINIUM; PLANNED UNIT DEVELOPMENT:**
   A. The Premises are a unit in a condominium, planned unit development, common interest subdivision or other development governed by a homeowners' association ("HOA"). The name of the HOA is _____ . Tenant agrees to comply with all HOA covenants, conditions and restrictions, bylaws, rules and regulations and decisions ("HOA Rules"). Landlord shall provide Tenant copies of HOA Rules, if any. Tenant shall reimburse Landlord for any fines or charges imposed by HOA or other authorities, due to any violation by Tenant, or the guests or licensees of Tenant.
   B. **(Check one)**
      ☐ 1. Landlord shall provide Tenant with a copy of the HOA Rules within _____ days or _____ .
      OR ☐ 2. Tenant has been provided with, and acknowledges receipt of, a copy of the HOA Rules.

7. **ALTERATIONS; REPAIRS:** Unless otherwise specified by law or paragraph 29C, without Landlord's prior written consent, (i) Tenant shall not make any repairs, alterations or improvements in or about the Premises including: painting, wallpapering, adding or changing locks, installing antenna or satellite dish(es), placing signs, displays or exhibits, or using screws, fastening devices, large nails or adhesive materials; (ii) Landlord shall not be responsible for the costs of alterations or repairs made by Tenant; (iii) Tenant shall not deduct from Rent the costs of any repairs, alterations or improvements; and (iv) any deduction made by Tenant shall be considered unpaid Rent.

8. **KEYS; LOCKS:**
   A. Tenant acknowledges receipt of (or Tenant will receive ☐ prior to the Commencement Date, or ☐ _____):
      ☐ _____ key(s) to Premises,   ☐ _____ remote control device(s) for garage door/gate opener(s),
      ☐ _____ key(s) to mailbox,   _____ ,
      ☐ _____ key(s) to common area(s),   _____ .
   B. Tenant acknowledges that locks to the Premises ☐ have ☐ have not, been re-keyed.
   C. If Tenant re-keys existing locks or opening devices, Tenant shall immediately deliver copies of all keys to Landlord. Tenant shall pay all costs and charges related to loss of any keys or opening devices. Tenant may not remove locks, even if installed by Tenant.

9. **ENTRY:**
   A. Tenant shall make Premises available to Landlord or Landlord's representative for the purpose of entering to make necessary or agreed repairs, (including, but not limited to, installing, repairing, testing, and maintaining smoke detectors and carbon monoxide devices, and bracing, anchoring or strapping water heaters), decorations, alterations, or improvements, or to supply necessary or agreed services, or to show Premises to prospective or actual purchasers, tenants, mortgagees, lenders, appraisers, or contractors.
   B. Landlord and Tenant agree that 24-hour written notice shall be reasonable and sufficient notice, except as follows: (1) 48-hour written notice is required to conduct an inspection of the Premises prior to the Tenant moving out, unless the Tenant waives the right to such notice. (2) If Landlord has in writing informed Tenant that the Premises are for sale and that Tenant will be notified orally to show the premises (C.A.R. Form NSE), then, for the next 120 days following the delivery of the NSE, notice may be given orally to show the Premises to actual or prospective purchasers. (3) No written notice is required if Landlord and Tenant orally agree to an entry for agreed services or repairs if the date and time of entry are within one week of the oral agreement. (4) No notice is required: (i) to enter in case of an emergency; (ii) if the Tenant is present and consents at the time of entry; or (iii) if the Tenant has abandoned or surrendered the Premises.
   C. ☐ (If checked) Tenant authorizes the use of a keysafe/lockbox to allow entry into the Premises and agrees to sign a keysafe/lockbox addendum (C.A.R. Form KLA).

10. **SIGNS:** Tenant authorizes Landlord to place FOR SALE/LEASE signs on the Premises.

11. **ASSIGNMENT; SUBLETTING:** Tenant shall not sublet all or any part of Premises, or assign or transfer this Agreement or any interest in it, without Landlord's prior written consent. Unless such consent is obtained, any assignment, transfer or subletting of Premises or this Agreement or tenancy, by voluntary act of Tenant, operation of law or otherwise, shall, at the option of Landlord, terminate this Agreement. Any proposed assignee, transferee or sublessee shall submit to Landlord an application and credit information for Landlord's approval and, if approved, sign a separate written agreement with Landlord and Tenant. Landlord's consent to any one assignment, transfer or sublease, shall not be construed as consent to any subsequent assignment, transfer or sublease and does not release Tenant of Tenant's obligations under this Agreement.

Tenant's Initials (_____) (_____)   Landlord's Initials (_____) (_____)

R REVISED 12/13 (PAGE 3 OF 6)

| Reviewed by _____ Date _____ |

RESIDENTIAL LEASE OR MONTH-TO-MONTH RENTAL AGREEMENT (LR PAGE 3 OF 6)

123 Sample street

Premises: _____ Date: _____

22. JOINT AND INDIVIDUAL OBLIGATIONS: If there is more than one Tenant, each one shall be individually and completely responsible for the performance of all obligations of Tenant under this Agreement, jointly with every other Tenant, and individually, whether or not in possession.

23. ☐ **LEAD-BASED PAINT (If checked):** Premises were constructed prior to 1978. In accordance with federal law, Landlord gives and Tenant acknowledges receipt of the disclosures on the attached form (C.A.R. Form FLD) and a federally approved lead pamphlet.

24. ☐ **MILITARY ORDNANCE DISCLOSURE:** (If applicable and known to Landlord) Premises are located within one mile of an area once used for military training, and may contain potentially explosive munitions.

25. ☐ **PERIODIC PEST CONTROL:** Landlord has entered into a contract for periodic pest control treatment of the Premises and shall give Tenant a copy of the notice originally given to Landlord by the pest control company.

26. ☐ **METHAMPHETAMINE CONTAMINATION:** Prior to signing this Agreement, Landlord has given Tenant a notice that a health official has issued an order prohibiting occupancy of the property because of methamphetamine contamination. A copy of the notice and order are attached.

27. MEGAN'S LAW DATABASE DISCLOSURE: Notice: Pursuant to Section 290.46 of the Penal Code, information about specified registered sex offenders is made available to the public via an Internet Web site maintained by the Department of Justice at www.meganslaw.ca.gov. Depending on an offender's criminal history, this information will include either the address at which the offender resides or the community of residence and ZIP Code in which he or she resides. (Neither Landlord nor Brokers, if any, are required to check this website. If Tenant wants further information, Tenant should obtain information directly from this website.)

28. POSSESSION:
    A. Tenant is not in possession of the Premises. If Landlord is unable to deliver possession of Premises on Commencement Date, such Date shall be extended to the date on which possession is made available to Tenant. If Landlord is unable to deliver possession within **5 (or** ☐ _____ **) calendar days** after agreed Commencement Date, Tenant may terminate this Agreement by giving written notice to Landlord, and shall be refunded all Rent and security deposit paid. Possession is deemed terminated when Tenant has returned all keys to the Premises to Landlord.
    B. ☐ Tenant is already in possession of the Premises.

29. TENANT'S OBLIGATIONS UPON VACATING PREMISES:
    A. Upon termination of this Agreement, Tenant shall: **(i)** give Landlord all copies of all keys or opening devices to Premises including any common areas; **(ii)** vacate and surrender Premises to Landlord, empty of all persons; **(iii)** vacate any and all parking and/or storage space; **(iv)** clean and deliver Premises, as specified in paragraph C below, to Landlord in the same condition as referenced in paragraph 10; **(v)** remove all debris; **(vi)** give written notice to Landlord of Tenant's forwarding address; and **(vii)** _____
    B. All alterations/improvements made by or caused to be made by Tenant, with or without Landlord's consent, become the property of Landlord upon termination. Landlord may charge Tenant for restoration of the Premises to the condition it was in prior to any alterations/improvements.
    C. Right to Pre-Move-Out Inspection and Repairs: (i) After giving or receiving notice of termination of a tenancy (C.A.R. Form NTT), or before the end of a lease, Tenant has the right to request that an inspection of the Premises take place prior to termination of the lease or rental (C.A.R. Form NRI). If Tenant requests such an inspection, Tenant shall be given an opportunity to remedy identified deficiencies prior to termination, consistent with the terms of this Agreement. **(ii)** Any repairs or alterations made to the Premises as a result of this inspection (collectively, "Repairs") shall be made at Tenant's expense. Repairs may be performed by Tenant or through others, who have adequate insurance and licenses and are approved by Landlord. The work shall comply with applicable law, including governmental permit, inspection and approval requirements. Repairs shall be performed in a good, skillful manner with materials of quality and appearance comparable to existing materials. It is understood that exact restoration of appearance or cosmetic items following all Repairs may not be possible. **(iii)** Tenant shall: **(a)** obtain receipts for Repairs performed by others; **(b)** prepare a written statement indicating the Repairs performed by Tenant and the date of such Repairs; and **(c)** provide copies of receipts and statements to Landlord prior to termination. Paragraph 29C does not apply when the tenancy is terminated pursuant to California Code of Civil Procedure § 1161(2), (3) or (4).

30. BREACH OF CONTRACT; EARLY TERMINATION: In addition to any obligations established by paragraph 29, in the event of termination by Tenant prior to completion of the original term of the Agreement, Tenant shall also be responsible for lost Rent, rental commissions, advertising expenses and painting costs necessary to ready Premises for re-rental. Landlord may withhold any such amounts from Tenant's security deposit.

31. TEMPORARY RELOCATION: Subject to local law, Tenant agrees, upon demand of Landlord, to temporarily vacate Premises for a reasonable period, to allow for fumigation (or other methods) to control wood destroying pests or organisms, or other repairs to Premises. Tenant agrees to comply with all instructions and requirements necessary to prepare Premises to accommodate pest control, fumigation or other work, including bagging or storage of food and medicine, and removal of perishables and valuables. Tenant shall only be entitled to a credit of Rent equal to the per diem Rent for the period of time Tenant is required to vacate Premises.

32. DAMAGE TO PREMISES: If, through no fault of Tenant, Premises are totally or partially damaged or destroyed by fire, earthquake, accident or other casualty that render Premises totally or partially uninhabitable, either Landlord or Tenant may terminate this Agreement by giving the other written notice. Rent shall be abated as of the date Premises become totally or partially uninhabitable. The abated amount shall be the current monthly Rent prorated on a 30-day period. If the Agreement is not terminated, Landlord shall promptly repair the damage, and Rent shall be reduced based on the extent to which the damage interferes with Tenant's reasonable use of Premises. If damage occurs as a result of an act of Tenant or Tenant's guests, only Landlord shall have the right of termination, and no reduction in Rent shall be made.

33. INSURANCE: Tenant's or guest's personal property and vehicles are not insured by Landlord, manager or, if applicable, HOA, against loss or damage due to fire, theft, vandalism, rain, water, criminal or negligent acts of others, or any other cause. **Tenant is advised to carry Tenant's own insurance (renter's insurance) to protect Tenant from any such loss or damage.** Tenant shall comply with any requirement imposed on Tenant by Landlord's insurer to avoid: **(i)** an increase in Landlord's insurance premium (or Tenant shall pay for the increase in premium); or **(ii)** loss of insurance.

34. WATERBEDS: Tenant shall not use or have waterbeds on the Premises unless: **(i)** Tenant obtains a valid waterbed insurance policy; **(ii)** Tenant increases the security deposit in an amount equal to one-half of one month's Rent; and **(iii)** the bed conforms to the floor load capacity of Premises.

35. WAIVER: The waiver of any breach shall not be construed as a continuing waiver of the same or any subsequent breach.

Tenant's Initials (_____) (_____)   Landlord's Initials (_____) (_____)

LR REVISED 12/13 (PAGE 4 OF 6) | Reviewed by _____ Date _____ |

RESIDENTIAL LEASE OR MONTH-TO-MONTH RENTAL AGREEMENT (LR PAGE 4 OF 6)

123 Sample street

mises: _____ Date: _____

NOTICE: Notices may be served at the following address, or at any other location subsequently designated:

Landlord: _____ Tenant: _____

_____   _____

_____   _____

TENANT ESTOPPEL CERTIFICATE: Tenant shall execute and return a tenant estoppel certificate delivered to Tenant by Landlord or Landlord's agent within **3 days** after its receipt. Failure to comply with this requirement shall be deemed Tenant's acknowledgment that the tenant estoppel certificate is true and correct, and may be relied upon by a lender or purchaser.

REPRESENTATION:

A. TENANT REPRESENTATION; OBLIGATIONS REGARDING OCCUPANTS; CREDIT: Tenant warrants that all statements in Tenant's rental application are accurate. Landlord requires all occupants 18 years of age or older and all emancipated minors to complete a lease rental application. Tenant acknowledges this requirement and agrees to notify Landlord when any occupant of the Premises reaches the age of 18 or becomes an emancipated minor. Tenant authorizes Landlord and Broker(s) to obtain Tenant's credit report periodically during the tenancy in connection with the modification or enforcement of this Agreement. Landlord may cancel this Agreement: **(i)** before occupancy begins; **(ii)** upon disapproval of the credit report(s); or **(iii)** at any time, upon discovering that information in Tenant's application is false. A negative credit report reflecting on Tenant's record may be submitted to a credit reporting agency if Tenant fails to fulfill the terms of payment and other obligations under this Agreement.

B. LANDLORD REPRESENTATIONS: Landlord warrants, that unless otherwise specified in writing, Landlord is unaware of **(i)** any recorded Notices of Default affecting the Premise; **(ii)** any delinquent amounts due under any loan secured by the Premises; and **(iii)** any bankruptcy proceeding affecting the Premises.

MEDIATION:

A. Consistent with paragraphs B and C below, Landlord and Tenant agree to mediate any dispute or claim arising between them out of this Agreement, or any resulting transaction, before resorting to court action. Mediation fees, if any, shall be divided equally among the parties involved. If, for any dispute or claim to which this paragraph applies, any party commences an action without first attempting to resolve the matter through mediation, or refuses to mediate after a request has been made, then that party shall not be entitled to recover attorney fees, even if they would otherwise be available to that party in any such action.

B. The following matters are excluded from mediation: **(i)** an unlawful detainer action; **(ii)** the filing or enforcement of a mechanic's lien; and **(iii)** any matter within the jurisdiction of a probate, small claims or bankruptcy court. The filing of a court action to enable the recording of a notice of pending action, for order of attachment, receivership, injunction, or other provisional remedies, shall not constitute a waiver of the mediation provision.

C. Landlord and Tenant agree to mediate disputes or claims involving Listing Agent, Leasing Agent or property manager ("Broker"), provided Broker shall have agreed to such mediation prior to, or within a reasonable time after, the dispute or claim is presented to such Broker. Any election by Broker to participate in mediation shall not result in Broker being deemed a party to this Agreement.

ATTORNEY FEES: In any action or proceeding arising out of this Agreement, the prevailing party between Landlord and Tenant shall be entitled to reasonable attorney fees and costs, except as provided in paragraph 39A.

C.A.R. FORM: C.A.R. Form means the specific form referenced or another comparable form agreed to by the parties.

OTHER TERMS AND CONDITIONS; SUPPLEMENTS: ☐ Interpreter/Translator Agreement (C.A.R. Form ITA);

☐ Keysafe/Lockbox Addendum (C.A.R. Form KLA); ☐ Lead-Based Paint and Lead-Based Paint Hazards Disclosure (C.A.R. Form FLD);

☐ Landlord in Default Addendum (C.A.R. Form LID) _____

The following ATTACHED supplements are incorporated in this Agreement. _____

_____

TIME OF ESSENCE; ENTIRE CONTRACT; CHANGES: Time is of the essence. All understandings between the parties are incorporated in this Agreement. Its terms are intended by the parties as a final, complete and exclusive expression of their Agreement with respect to its subject matter, and may not be contradicted by evidence of any prior agreement or contemporaneous oral agreement. If any provision of this Agreement is held to be ineffective or invalid, the remaining provisions will nevertheless be given full force and effect. Neither this Agreement nor any provision in it may be extended, amended, modified, altered or changed except in writing. This Agreement is subject to California landlord-tenant law and shall incorporate all changes required by amendment or successors to such law. This Agreement and any supplement, addendum or modification, including any copy, may be signed in two or more counterparts, all of which shall constitute one and the same writing.

AGENCY:

A. CONFIRMATION: The following agency relationship(s) are hereby confirmed for this transaction:

Listing Agent: (Print firm name _____

is the agent of (check one): ☐ the Landlord exclusively; or ☐ both the Landlord and Tenant.

Leasing Agent: (Print firm name _____

(if not same as Listing Agent) is the agent of (check one): ☐ the Tenant exclusively; or ☐ the Landlord exclusively; or ☐ both the Tenant and Landlord.

B. DISCLOSURE: ☐ (If checked): The term of this lease exceeds one year. A disclosure regarding real estate agency relationships (C.A.R. Form AD) has been provided to Landlord and Tenant, who each acknowledge its receipt.

☐ **TENANT COMPENSATION TO BROKER:** Upon execution of this Agreement, Tenant agrees to pay compensation to Broker as specified in a separate written agreement between Tenant and Broker.

Tenant's Initials (_____) (_____)   Landlord's Initials (_____) (_____)

| Reviewed by _____ Date _____ |

EQUAL HOUSING OPPORTUNITY

REVISED 12/13 (PAGE 5 OF 6)

RESIDENTIAL LEASE OR MONTH-TO-MONTH RENTAL AGREEMENT (LR PAGE 5 OF 6)

Michael Wolf

123 Sample street

Premises: _____ Date: _____

46. ☐ **INTERPRETER/TRANSLATOR:** The terms of this Agreement have been interpreted for Tenant into the following language _____ . Landlord and Tenant acknowledge receipt the attached interpreter/translator agreement (C.A.R. Form ITA).

47. FOREIGN LANGUAGE NEGOTIATION: If this Agreement has been negotiated by Landlord and Tenant primarily in Spanish Chinese, Tagalog, Korean or Vietnamese, pursuant to the California Civil Code, Tenant shall be provided a translation of Agreement in the language used for the negotiation.

48. OWNER COMPENSATION TO BROKER: Upon execution of this Agreement, Owner agrees to pay compensation to Broker specified in a separate written agreement between Owner and Broker (C.A.R. Form LCA).

49. RECEIPT: If specified in paragraph 5, Landlord or Broker, acknowledges receipt of move-in funds.

Landlord and Tenant acknowledge and agree Brokers: **(a)** do not guarantee the condition of the Premises; **(b)** cannot verify representations made by others; **(c)** cannot provide legal or tax advice; **(d)** will not provide other advice or information that exceeds the knowledge, education or experience required to obtain a real estate license. Furthermore, if Brokers are not also acting as Landlord in this Agreement, Brokers: **(e)** do not decide what rental rate a Tenant should pay or Landlord should accept; and **(f)** do not decide upon the length or other terms of tenancy. Landlord and Tenant agree that they will seek legal, tax, insurance and other desired assistance from appropriate professionals.

Tenant agrees to rent the Premises on the above terms and conditions.

Tenant _____ Date _____
Address _____ City _____ State _____ Zip _____
Telephone _____ Fax _____ E-mail _____

Tenant _____ Date _____
Address _____ City _____ State _____ Zip _____
Telephone _____ Fax _____ E-mail _____

☐ **GUARANTEE:** In consideration of the execution of this Agreement by and between Landlord and Tenant and for valuable consideration, receipt of which is hereby acknowledged, the undersigned ("Guarantor") does hereby: **(i)** guarantee unconditionally to Landlord and Landlord's agents, successors and assigns, the prompt payment of Rent or other sums that become due pursuant to this Agreement, including any and all court costs and attorney fees included in enforcing the Agreement; **(ii)** consent to any changes, modifications or alterations of any term in this Agreement agreed to by Landlord and Tenant; and **(iii)** waive any right to require Landlord and/or Landlord's agents to proceed against Tenant for any default occurring under the Agreement before seeking to enforce this Guarantee.

Guarantor (Print Name) _____
Guarantor _____ Date _____
Address _____ City _____ State _____ Zip _____
Telephone _____ Fax _____ E-mail _____

Landlord agrees to rent the Premises on the above terms and conditions.

Landlord _____ Date _____ Landlord _____ Date _____

Address _____
Telephone _____ Fax _____ E-mail _____

REAL ESTATE BROKERS

A. Real estate brokers who are not also Landlord under this Agreement are not parties to the Agreement between Landlord and Tenant.

B. Agency relationships are confirmed in paragraph 44.

C. **COOPERATING BROKER COMPENSATION:** Listing Broker agrees to pay Cooperating Broker (Leasing Firm) and Cooperating Broker agrees to accept: **(i)** the amount specified in the MLS, provided Cooperating Broker is a Participant of the MLS in which the Property is offered for sale or a reciprocal MLS; or **(ii)** ☐ (if checked) the amount specified in a separate written agreement between Listing Broker and Cooperating Broker.

Real Estate Broker (Listing Firm) _____ BRE Lic. # _____
By (Agent) _____ BRE Lic. # _____ Date _____
Address _____ City _____ State _____ Zip _____
Telephone _____ Fax _____ E-mail _____

Real Estate Broker (Leasing Firm) _____ BRE Lic. # _____
By (Agent) _____ BRE Lic. # _____ Date _____
Address _____ City _____ State _____ Zip _____
Telephone _____ Fax _____ E-mail _____

Reviewed by _____ Date _____

LR REVISED 12/13 (PAGE 6 OF 6)

RESIDENTIAL LEASE OR MONTH-TO-MONTH RENTAL AGREEMENT (LR PAGE 6 OF 6)

CALIFORNIA
ASSOCIATION
OF REALTORS®

APPLICATION TO RENT/SCREENING FEE
(C.A.R. Form LRA, Revised 11/13)

I. APPLICATION TO RENT

THIS SECTION TO BE COMPLETED BY APPLICANT. A SEPARATE APPLICATION TO RENT IS REQUIRED FOR EACH OCCUPANT 18 YEARS OF AGE OR OVER, OR AN EMANCIPATED MINOR.

1. Applicant is completing Application as a (check one) ☐ tenant, ☐ tenant with co-tenant(s) or ☐ guarantor/co-signor. Total number of applicants _____ .

2. **PREMISES INFORMATION**
Application to rent property at _____ 123 Sample street, , _____ ("Premises")
Rent: $ _____ per _____ Proposed move-in date _____

3. **PERSONAL INFORMATION**
A. FULL NAME OF APPLICANT _____
B. Date of Birth _____ (For purpose of obtaining credit reports. Age discrimination is prohibited by law.)
C. Social Security No. _____ Driver's License No. _____
State _____ Expires _____
D. Phone Number: Home_____ Work _____ Other _____
E. Email _____
F. Name(s) of all other proposed occupant(s) and relationship to applicant _____
_____
G. Pet(s) or service animals (number and type) _____
H. Auto: Make _____ Model _____ Year _____ License No. _____ State _____ Color _____
Other vehicle(s): _____
I. In case of emergency, person to notify _____
Relationship _____
Address _____ Phone _____
J. Does applicant or any proposed occupant plan to use liquid-filled furniture? ☐ No ☐ Yes Type _____
K. Has applicant been a party to an unlawful detainer action or filed bankruptcy within the last seven years? ☐ No ☐ Yes
If yes, explain _____
L. Has applicant or any proposed occupant ever been convicted of or pleaded no contest to a felony?   ☐ No ☐ Yes
If yes, explain _____
M. Has applicant or any proposed occupant ever been asked to move out of a residence?   ☐ No ☐ Yes
If yes, explain _____

4. **RESIDENCE HISTORY**

Current address	Previous address
City/State/Zip	City/State/Zip
From _____ to _____	From _____ to _____
Name of Landlord/Manager	Name of Landlord/Manager
Landlord/Manager's phone	Landlord/Manager's phone
Do you own this property? ☐ No ☐ Yes	Did you own this property? ☐ No ☐ Yes
Reason for leaving current address	Reason for leaving this address

5. **EMPLOYMENT AND INCOME HISTORY**

Current employer	Previous employer
Current employer address	Prev. employer address
From _____ To _____	From _____ To _____
Supervisor	Supervisor
Supervisor phone	Supervisor phone
Employment gross income $_____ per _____	Employment gross income $_____ per _____
Other income info	Other income info

Applicant's Initials (_____) (_____)

Reviewed by _____ Date _____

EQUAL HOUSING OPPORTUNITY

LRA REVISED 11/13 (PAGE 1 OF 2)

APPLICATION TO RENT/SCREENING FEE (LRA PAGE 1 OF 2)

Agent: Michael Wolf	**Phone:** 858-722-6847	**Fax:** 619-923-3201	Prepared using zipForm® software
Broker: Ascent Real Estate Inc,410 Kalmia	San Diego	,CA 92101	

Property Address: *123 Sample street, ,* Date: _____

6. CREDIT INFORMATION

Name of creditor	Account number	Monthly payment	Balance due

Name of bank/branch	Account number	Type of account	Account balance

7. PERSONAL REFERENCES

Name _____ Address _____

Phone _____ Length of acquaintance _____ Occupation _____

Name _____ Address _____

Phone _____ Length of acquaintance _____ Occupation _____

8. NEAREST RELATIVE(S)

Name _____ Address _____

Phone _____ Relationship _____

Name _____ Address _____

Phone _____ Relationship _____

Applicant understands and agrees that: **(i)** this is an application to rent only and does not guarantee that applicant will be offered the Premises; **(ii)** Landlord or Manager or Agent may accept more than one application for the Premises and, using their sole discretion, will select the best qualified applicant, and **(iii)** Applicant will provide a copy of applicant's driver's license upon request.

Applicant represents the above information to be true and complete, and hereby authorizes Landlord or Manager or Agent to: **(i)** verify the information provided; and **(ii)** obtain a credit report on applicant and other reports, warnings and verifications on and about applicant, which may include, but not be limited to, criminal background checks, reports on unlawful detainers, bad checks, fraud warnings, employment and tenant history. Applicant further authorizes Landlord or Manager or Agent to disclose information to prior or subsequent owners and/or agents.

If application is not fully completed, or received without the screening fee: (i) the application will not be processed, and (ii) the application and any screening fee will be returned.

Applicant _____ Date _____ Time _____

Return your completed application and any applicable fee not already paid to: _____

Address _____ City _____ State _____ Zip _____

II. SCREENING FEE

THIS SECTION TO BE COMPLETED BY LANDLORD, MANAGER OR AGENT.

Applicant has paid a **nonrefundable** screening fee of $ _____ , applied as follows: (The screening fee may not exceed $30.00, adjusted annually from 1-1-98 commensurate with the increase in the Consumer Price Index. A CPI inflation calculator is available on the Bureau of Labor Statistics website, www.bls.gov. The California Department of Consumer Affairs calculates the applicable screening fee amount to be $42.06 as of 2009.)

$ _____ for credit reports prepared by _____ ;

$ _____ for _____ (other out-of-pocket expenses); and

$ _____ for processing.

The undersigned has read the foregoing and acknowledges receipt of a copy.

_____ Date _____
Applicant Signature

The undersigned has received the screening fee indicated above.

_____ CalBRE Lic. # _____
Landlord or Manager or Agent Signature Date _____

Reviewed by _____ Date _____

LRA REVISED 11/13 (PAGE 2 OF 2)

APPLICATION TO RENT/SCREENING FEE (LRA PAGE 2 OF 2) rental app and lease

GLOSSARY

Frequently Used Terms for Investment Property Analysis

1031 Exchange: Under Section 1031 of the IRS Tax Code, like-kind property used in a trade or business or held as an investment can be exchanged tax-free, subject to certain conditions.

Before-Tax Cash Flow: Before-tax cash flow is what the investor will keep after covering all costs, but before the payment of income taxes. Basically, it's the net cash flow for the investor before he pays taxes. Before-tax cash flow is the result when the annual debt service is subtracted from the net operating income.

CAP RATE: Capitalization rate (or "CAP rate") is the ratio between the net operating income produced by an asset and its capital cost (the original price paid to buy the asset) or alternatively its current market value.

Cash Flow: The net operating income minus the total of all debt service payments. (See definition of "net operating income" below.)

Debt Coverage Ratio (DCR): A ratio used in underwriting loans for income producing property, which is created by dividing net operating income by total debt service. Ratios of at least 1.10 are generally required with ratios of 1.20 and higher considered the norm. (See definition of "underwriting" below.).

Deferred Maintenance: A type of physical depreciation due to lack of normal upkeep.

Depreciation Recapture: When real property is sold at a gain and accelerated depreciation has been claimed, the owner may be required to pay tax at ordinary income rates to the extent of the excess accelerated depreciation.

Dollars Lost: Vacancies do not generate revenue. The "dollars lost" figure is the vacancy factor applied to the gross scheduled income, and will decrease it.

Estoppel: A doctrine of law that stops one from later denying facts, which that person once acknowledged were true and others accepted on good faith.

Eviction: Legal proceeding by a lessor (landlord) to recover possession of property.

Gross Operating Income: Gross Operating Income is the result when other income is added to rental income.

Gross Rent Multiplier: A way to quickly compare and compute the value of income producing properties in similar locations. The GRM is the sales price divided by the gross annual rent or gross scheduled income (GSI).

Gross Scheduled Income (GSI): Gross Scheduled Income is the maximum amount of rent the owner could potentially receive on the property. (i.e., if the property were 100% occupied at either contract rents or market rents for 100% of the year).

Internal Rate of Return (IRR): Is a rate of return or yield used in capital budgeting to measure and compare the profitability of investment capital each year it remains invested in the investment. Generally speaking, the higher a project's IRR, the more desirable it is to undertake the project. A simple way to compute and to compare is to use the annual cash flows during a given period of time, (return on investment) divided by initial investment or sale price to calculate yield.

Lease: A contract in which, for a rent payment, the one entitled to the possession of the real property (lessor or landlord) transfers those rights to another (lessee) for a specified period of time

Loan-to-Value (LTV): The ratio of the size of the loan to the value of the property. If the loan is $80,000 and the value of the property is $100,000 the LTV is 80% ($80,000 / $100,000).

Management Agreement: A contract between the owner of property and someone who agrees to manage it.

Negative Before-Tax Cash Flow: If the annual debt service is larger than the net operating income, the property will produce a negative before tax cash flow.

Net Operating Income: Net Operating Income is the result when annual operating expenses are subtracted from gross operating income. Net operating income is a key figure in cash flow analysis. First, it is the amount of money the property is estimated to produce to cover the loan payments for the year; and second, net operating income is used by investors and appraisers to estimate the price or value of the property. Loan payments are not considered an annual operating expense to run a property. They are a financial cost to an owner who chooses to borrow rather than pay cash, but they are not considered an operating expense.

PITI: The shorthand way of stating the most usual elements of a residential mortgage payment, which may consist not only of the Principal and Interest (PI), but also the property taxes (T) and hazard insurance (I) as well. In the case where all four elements are part of the payment, the lender escrows the (T) and (I) and pays them on behalf of the borrower when they come due. Some loans are written such that the payment to the lender consists only of the (P) and (I) in which case the borrower pays the taxes and insurance directly.

Security Deposit: Cash payment required by landlord to be held during the term of the lease to offset damages incurred due to actions of the tenant.

Triple Net Lease: Lease in which the tenant is to pay all operating expenses of the property so that the landlord receives net rent, frequently used to mean tenant pays taxes, insurance, and maintenance in addition to normal operating expenses

Vacancy & Uncollected Rent Rate: This rate is expressed as a percentage, and is an allowance or discount for estimated vacancies (units not rented) in a rental property. The vacancy rate is converted to dollars lost. In other words, the higher the vacancy rate the lower the cash flow.

*CREDIT: GOOGLE, WIKIPEDIA, reiclub.com, Investment Property Analysis.

ABOUT THE AUTHOR

For over a decade, I've been blessed to live my passion as a professional realtor helping my clients buy, sell, and invest in real estate. Along with my wife Jessica, I co-founded The Wolf Real Estate Group in 2006. Together, it has been our commitment to support our clients with accurate information and knowledge that will help them make good choices with their investments.

In working with many of our first-time homebuyers, I was compelled to help offer them the information they need to make good decisions and avoid pitfalls when buying their first home. So, in 2010, I published *The First Time Homebuyer Book* to help guide first time homebuyers with the biggest purchase decision of their lives.

Over the years, it has become apparent that learning how to protect and grow that investment can be challenging as well. My latest book, *The First Time Home Investor Book* helps homeowners and investors grow their wealth through investment real estate. It is created to share investment information and offer the critically important steps to becoming financially independent for the first time investor.

Writing these books for our clients and serving on multiple committees within the local San Diego Association of Realtors is important to me; it offers my wife and I the opportunity to give back to my community and usher in a fresh and positive perspectives for the future of real estate.

It is so rewarding to empower my clients and offer my expertise and knowledge to them as they build their financial futures. I'm committed to supporting them in all aspects of real estate sales, structuring investments, and representing all my buyers and sellers with their residential and investment properties. I believe our future is bright and I am passionate about doing my part to empower people one relationship at a time.

CPSIA information can be obtained
at www.ICGtesting.com
Printed in the USA
BVOW11s1919310817

493541BV00011B/170/P